IT ACTUALLY HAPPENED

TRUE STORIES OF THE WORLD'S MOST NOTORIOUS THIEVES

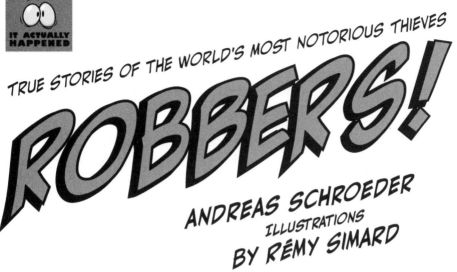

ROBBERS!

ANDREAS SCHROEDER

ILLUSTRATIONS
BY RÊMY SIMARD

annick press
toronto + new york + vancouver

This book is the second in the It Actually Happened series.

(text) © 2012 Andreas Schroeder

(artwork) © 2012 Rémy Simard

Edited by Catherine Marjoribanks

Proofread by Tanya Trafford

ANNICK PRESS LTD.

We acknowledge the support of the Canada Council for the Arts, the Ontario Arts Council, and the Government of Canada through the Canada Book Fund (CBF) for our publishing activities.

 ONTARIO ARTS COUNCIL
CONSEIL DES ARTS DE L'ONTARIO

CATALOGING IN PUBLICATION

Schroeder, Andreas, 1946-

    Robbers! : true stories of the world's most notorious thieves / Andreas Schroeder ; illustrations by Rémy Simard.

(It actually happened series)
Includes bibliographical references and index.
ISBN 978-1-55451-441-0 (bound).—ISBN 978-1-55451-440-3 (pbk.)

    1. Robbery—Juvenile literature. 2. Theft—Juvenile literature.
3. Thieves—Juvenile literature. I. Simard, Rémy II. Title.
III. Series: It actually happened series

HV6652.S355 2012   j364.15'52   C2012-902080-X

Published in the U.S.A. by
Annick Press (U.S.) Ltd.

Distributed in Canada by
Firefly Books Ltd.
66 Leek Crescent
P.O. Box 1338
Richmond Hill, ON
L4B 1H1

Distributed in the U.S.A. by
Firefly Books (U.S.) Inc.
P.O. Box 1338
Ellicott Station
Buffalo, NY 14205

Printed and bound in Canada

Visit our website at **www.annickpress.com**
Visit Andreas Schroeder at **www.apschroeder.com**
Visit Rémy Simard at **www.remysimard.com**

 MIX
Paper from
responsible sources
FSC® C004071

CONTENTS

2 INTRODUCTION: TRYING FOR THE BIG SCORE

6 ON THE RUN WITH MONA LISA

28 BLOWING THE VAULT AT LAGUNA NIGUEL

48 TAKE THE MONEY AND FLY

70 THE NAPOLEON OF CRIME

90 BANKNOTES FROM HEAVEN

104 THE CLASSIEST THIEF IN MANHATTAN

126 THE GREAT TRAIN ROBBERY

144 THE MANY FACES OF WILLIE SUTTON

162 BIBLIOGRAPHY

164 INDEX

166 FURTHER READING

166 ABOUT THE AUTHOR AND ILLUSTRATOR

INTRODUCTION
TRYING FOR THE BIG SCORE

Stealing is probably the most common of crimes. The impulse to simply take something we want—even if it belongs to someone else—can sometimes be irresistible.

Cassie Chadwick, who became one of North America's most notorious female embezzlers, stole from an early age: jewelry, cosmetics, clothes, even groceries. She was often caught, and she stole so much and so often that a judge eventually pronounced her insane. But that didn't stop her from making one last robbery, this time by tricking bankers into lending her large amounts of money based on her (phony) claim that she was going to inherit money from America's richest industrialist, Andrew Carnegie. For Cassie, it was like taking candy from a baby—why would she quit?

The problem for many robbers is that when they make a big score, they party, and blow their ill-gotten gains on huge mansions, flashy cars, or luxury yachts. But in order to spend a lot of money, you've got to keep stealing a lot of money. So a thief's life can become a treadmill—and when the police finally come knocking, that treadmill crashes. Any money left is usually taken by the lawyers. Almost always, thieves end their careers broke and disillusioned.

In the 1890s, Soapy Smith and his crew practically owned the town of Skagway, Alaska, which was the doorway to the Alaska gold rush. Every boat that arrived in Skagway was met by a "town official" who informed all the passengers that a decent haircut was a legal sanitary requirement in Skagway. As the passengers sat in their barber chairs, the barbers (who were also on Soapy's payroll) grilled them for information.

Generally, robbers cause everyone a great deal of grief and misery. But now and then there are robbers who steal to help others, or to draw attention to injustice. In Australia, Ned Kelly was a sort of nineteenth-century Robin Hood. Farmers there were angry because rich landowners were taking over all the best farmland, and so Ned Kelly saw nothing wrong with taking the odd cow or horse from people who, in his view, had themselves stolen half the surrounding countryside.

SOON NED, WITH A SMALL GANG OF LIKE-MINDED FRIENDS, WAS ON THE RUN, ROAMING THE COUNTRYSIDE AND ROBBING BANKS FOR POCKET MONEY. WHEN NED WAS FINALLY CAUGHT AND HANGED FOR HIS CRIMES, HE BECAME A SYMBOL OF COURAGE, RECKLESSNESS, AND THE REFUSAL TO BE PUSHED AROUND BY CORRUPT OFFICIALDOM.

And then, sometimes, a successful robber might end up sharing his loot Robin Hood style, whether he likes it or not. Joe Weil, nicknamed "The Yellow Kid" after a popular comic strip character, was one of America's most successful robbers in the 1920s and '30s. When he decided to retire, he invested his ill-gotten gains in a legitimate hotel. But as soon as Weil's friends heard about his hotel, they all showed up at his door and made it their favorite hangout. It became so notorious for its crooked clientele that law-abiding people stopped patronizing the place. Meanwhile, Weil's friends weren't paying their bills.

"Your thieving friends are robbing you blind!" his wife complained, and it was true. Weil's hotel soon went broke, and so did Weil. He wound up living off his wife's store-clerk salary.

The eight stories that follow are taken from a wide variety of documented sources. They all happened within the past 150 years, and most of them involve professional robbers who spent their lives figuring out ingenious ways to steal other people's possessions.

Some of these robbers were more talented than others, so some of the stories are perhaps funnier than their perpetrators intended. Some are heart-warming, and some are heart-breaking. Any one of these robbers could be a character in a movie or TV show—some of them already are. And all of the stories share one common characteristic: they make for great reading.

ON THE RUN WITH MONA LISA

Was it theft, or rescuing a national treasure? The police had no doubts!

THE ROBBERS

Vincenzo Perugia and his sidekicks

On a Sunday afternoon, August 20, 1911, three Italian workmen joined the crowds swarming eagerly through the vast Musée du Louvre in Paris, trying very hard to look like tourists. After all, the Louvre, France's most renowned art museum, was a popular tourist attraction, with more than two hundred galleries displaying thousands of the world's most famous and valuable paintings.

The three men sauntered through gallery after gallery, casually following the crowds. Here and there, they paused, pretending to study the magnificent paintings.

But these "tourists" were actually Vincenzo Perugia, a cabinet-maker, and his partners, the Lancelotti brothers—and they weren't there to admire the art.

Perugia and the Lancelotti brothers waited until the last of the visitors had finally drifted out of the room. "Now!" Perugia hissed. He reached behind a large painting by Bramantino and pushed on a hidden spring in the wall. A narrow door opened inward behind the painting, revealing a small storeroom.

From the other galleries, they could still hear the faint voices of the guards making their rounds, herding the last remaining tourists toward the front door.

THE THREE MEN SLIPPED
INSIDE AND CLOSED THE DOOR.

A NIGHT AT THE MUSEUM
Hiding out before the big heist

The next morning, the three men awoke to the sound of shuffling footsteps and the clatter of a cleaner's cart outside the storeroom door. On Mondays, the Louvre was closed to the public for maintenance and repairs. Instead of tourists, an army of cleaners, electricians, plumbers, carpenters, and plasterers swarmed through the museum. They were all dressed in loose, white, museum-issue smocks, which served as both uniform and identity card. Anyone wearing such a smock on Mondays at the Louvre was obviously a museum employee.

Perugia and his accomplices drew identical white smocks from under their jackets and pulled them on over their street clothes. They waited until the steps had faded away and then opened the door a crack. They were in luck—the gallery was empty.

The brothers quickly picked up a broom and a mop they found leaning against one of the walls. Perugia pulled a dusting cloth out of his pocket. Dressed as maintenance crew, they proceeded to sweep and mop and dust their way from room to room, heading steadily toward one gallery—and one painting—in particular.

The Louvre had quite a few storerooms and hidden alcoves—even museum officials weren't sure how many. Some of these were used to store the easels, canvases, and art supplies of students who came to the gallery to copy the works of the Old Masters.

THE TARGET

A masterpiece

The painting they were after was in the Salon Carré, and it was the most famous portrait in the world: Leonardo da Vinci's *Mona Lisa*.

Several years earlier, Vincenzo Perugia had been employed by the Louvre to build vandal-resistant glass coverings for some of the museum's most valuable paintings. He had taken the job because he'd been desperate for work, but the assignment had appalled him. Imagine! Imprisoning the *Mona Lisa* in a cage! These crazy Frenchmen simply had no appreciation for fine Italian art. In fact, they didn't deserve the *Mona Lisa*!

AND THERE SHE WAS. IT WAS ENOUGH TO MAKE AN ITALIAN HOMESICK.

THE HEIST
Just look busy!

Earlier that morning, at about 7:20 a.m., the Louvre's maintenance director had gone through the Salon Carré with a co-worker, making his usual rounds. He'd stopped and pointed out to the other man that Leonardo's *Mona Lisa* was the most valuable object in the museum: "They say it is worth a million and a half!"

An obvious target for a robber? But no one was suspicious when Vincenzo Perugia and the Lancelotti brothers approached the painting. They seemed to be doing just what maintenance workers were doing all over the Louvre—taking down paintings for rearranging, repair, restoration, or reframing. No one challenged their actions. No one demanded an explanation.

The *Mona Lisa* was painted by Italian Leonardo da Vinci between 1503 and 1506. It was rumored that Napoleon was the first to steal the *Mona Lisa*, but in fact Leonardo himself brought the painting to France, as a gift for the king, François I.

Who was Mona Lisa? Scholars have long debated the question, but the most likely candidate is a woman named Lisa Gherardini, who was married to a wealthy merchant of Florence, Francesco del Giocondo. The *Mona Lisa* is also known by the name *La Gioconda*, which means "the merry one" but is also a pun on Lisa's married name. And why is she smiling so enigmatically? That remains a mystery.

THE THIEVES LIFTED
THE WORLD'S MOST FAMOUS
PORTRAIT FROM THE WALL ...

AND CARRIED IT THROUGH
THE LOUVRE'S GALLERIES ...

AND OUT THROUGH A DOORWAY
INTO A SERVICE STAIRWAY.

Perugia began slashing frantically at the heavy tape that held the portrait in its vandal-proof frame. While one of the brothers began taking the frame apart with a small crowbar, the other went to work on the outside door with a duplicate key.

"*Mannagia!* This stupid key won't work!" he said.

Perugia handed off the portrait and tried the key. It slid into the lock easily, but refused to turn. Alarmed, he whipped out a screwdriver and began to take apart the lock. His hands trembled, and the screwdriver kept slipping off the screws. Finally the doorknob fell off and the face plate came loose.

"*Attenti!*" one of the Lancelotti brothers hissed. "Somebody's coming!"

The other brother lunged behind the stairs with the portrait.

The door above them opened and a workman carrying a plumber's toolkit came down the stairs. Halfway down, he noticed two annoyed-looking maintenance men standing at the outside door below.

"This stupid doorknob has fallen off and now we can't get out!" one of them shouted in disgust. "Everything in this place is falling apart!"

"*Du calme, messieurs,*" the plumber replied soothingly. These excitable Italians—always making everything into an opera. He slid his own key into the lock, turned it, and then used a pair of pliers to substitute for the missing doorknob. "I'll put it on the maintenance report for tomorrow," he said. "But for now, better leave the door ajar. Someone else might have the same problem."

He waved and went cheerfully on his way.

Two minutes later, the *Mona Lisa* was in a cab with three very excited Italians, heading for Perugia's apartment a few city blocks away.

THE DISCOVERY
Finding nothing

Amazingly, it was a full twenty-seven hours before the authorities at the Louvre realized that the *Mona Lisa* was missing.

Even then, they hoped it was just a mistake. Had someone taken her to the Reproduction Shop to be photographed? Had she been sent down to the Restoration Shop for cleaning? Was she simply "in transit" between different shops? In an institution as vast as the Louvre, there was plenty of room for things to be misplaced.

But by Wednesday, August 23, every corner of the Louvre had been examined several times over, and the disassembled frame had been discovered in the stairwell. There was no longer any doubt about it—the most famous portrait in the world, and France's most beloved cultural treasure, had been stolen.

At that point, all hell broke loose.

"UNIMAGINABLE!" was the one-word headline of the Paris newspaper *Le Matin.*

"INEXPLICABLE!" echoed other French morning newspapers. "INCROYABLE!"

"What audacious criminal, what mystifier, what manic collector, what insane lover, has committed this abduction?" demanded the editors of the magazine *L'Illustration.*

Within hours, orders were telegraphed from the highest levels of government, sealing France's borders.

HARBORS WERE CLOSED.

RAILWAY STATIONS WERE SHUT DOWN.

ALL OUTGOING TRAINS, SHIPS, AND VEHICLES WERE SEARCHED.

THE INVESTIGATION
How did this happen?

Police swarmed into the Louvre. Inquiries were launched. Heads rolled. The senior curator was fired. The Undersecretary for Fine Arts was forced to resign.

It was decided that the theft must have been an inside job. The Louvre was ordered to produce a list of everyone who had been an employee of the museum during the past five years. All persons on that list were to be interrogated by the police. Anyone with a police record was to be questioned especially thoroughly.

The Lancelotti brothers had never worked for the Louvre and had no police records. Perugia, however, qualified on both counts. He worked for the Louvre and had twice been arrested—once on a charge of attempted robbery, once for the illegal possession of a knife. So he had reason to worry.

> When it comes to fingerprints and thumbprints, not only are one person's prints different from anyone else's (even with identical twins), a left-hand print is different from a right-hand print, and each finger has a different print from all the others.

Worse, the police discovered a left thumbprint on the discarded frame in the stairwell. But for some reason, Perugia's police file contained only his right thumbprint—and opposing thumbprints are not identical. Plus, his employment record at the Louvre had been misfiled.

WHEN THE LOUVRE DISCOVERED THE MISFILING THREE MONTHS LATER, THE POLICE SHOWED UP AT PERUGIA'S DOOR.

BUT AFTER HOURS OF QUESTIONING, THE OFFICERS DID NOT ARREST HIM.

Perugia had been late for work the morning of the theft, but the police accepted his explanation—that he'd drunk too much the night before and slept in—and never suspected that he'd been busy that morning walking away with the painting. His name was checked off the list, and the investigation moved on.

What the interrogating officer hadn't realized was that he had been sitting less than an arm's length away from the *Mona Lisa*. Perugia had wrapped her in a linen cloth and hidden her in the false bottom he'd built into a wooden trunk.

And that's where she remained for the next two years.

THE THIEF BEHIND THE THIEF

"The Signore"

While the French police continued their increasingly desperate search for the *Mona Lisa*, Vincenzo Perugia became more confused and angry.

The problem was, Perugia understood amazingly little about this robbery.

Earlier that summer, an elegantly dressed gentleman had called at Perugia's rooming house and explained that he wished to hire Perugia for an undertaking that would earn him enough money for many years to come. He seemed to know all about the Italian carpenter, his job at the Louvre, his police record, and his growing bitterness toward the French.

The man proposed that Perugia steal the *Mona Lisa*—and he had the plan all worked out.

It was the Signore (as Perugia called him—the man had been careful never to disclose his name) who provided the smocks, the duplicate key, and the location of the hidden storeroom.

He spread out a blueprint of the Louvre on Perugia's bed and showed Perugia exactly what to do, every step of the way. All Perugia had to do was arrange for the help of the Lancelotti brothers and steal the portrait.

Perugia and the Lancelotti brothers would each be paid a sum equivalent to about five years' income as a first installment, with Perugia receiving a second installment in the same amount when "everything succeeded."

THE SIGNORE PAID EVERYONE AS AGREED, WHEN PERUGIA MET HIM TO HAND OVER THE PORTRAIT.

But to Perugia's astonishment, the Signore merely admired the painting for a short while, then rewrapped it in its linen cloth and instructed Perugia to keep it hidden in his apartment, "until it is required."

Perugia assumed that the Signore intended to ransom the portrait, selling it back to the Louvre for a hefty sum. But as the months passed, there was no sign that any negotiations were taking place, and the police kept up their relentless dragnet efforts to find the painting.

Meanwhile, Vincenzo Perugia was broke once again, and still waiting for his second installment. He was also getting the distinct impression that he had somehow been fooled.

Finally, an idea occurred to him. He would take the *Mona Lisa* home to Italy. The French didn't deserve her. Only Italians could fully appreciate her. She belonged among her own kind, her own people, in a splendid art gallery in Milan, or maybe Florence.

THE TAKE-DOWN

Thief or national hero?

Perugia had recently come across an ad in a Florence newspaper: "Artworks of all kinds purchased for good prices." He would reply to that ad. He suspected that, unlike the stingy French, the Italians would probably pay a very good price for the *Mona Lisa*.

When Alfredo Geri, the gallery owner who had placed the ad, received Vincenzo Perugia's letter, he was sure that it had to be a joke. But Geri knew that the French police had completely run out of clues, and that several French organizations had posted enormous rewards. What did he have to lose?

One month, two letters, and three telegrams later, Alfredo Geri and Giovanni Poggi, director of Florence's world-famous Uffizi Gallery, stared in amazement as Perugia unwrapped the *Mona Lisa* in a smelly little hotel room in Florence.

Famous works of art are generally easy to steal, but very hard to sell. After all, if a dishonest collector buys a stolen Van Gogh, he can't exactly pretend he doesn't know where it came from. For that reason, about half the famous artworks that are stolen eventually find their way home again. Sometimes the robber holds the artwork for ransom; sometimes he returns it for an advertised reward, which might be offered by the owner or by the company insuring the painting.

Geri and Poggi examined the portrait wordlessly for some minutes.

"Signore Perugia," Geri said carefully, "how much are you asking for this painting?"

Perugia shrugged again. "Five hundred thousand lire?" It was an amount equivalent to about one hundred thousand dollars.

The two men smiled faintly. "We'll have the money for you by this afternoon," Geri said. "Please remain with the painting until then."

Perugia grinned happily. Clearly, Italians appreciated art far more than the French.

He probably felt a little differently half an hour later when the Florence police—alerted by Geri and Poggi—arrested him for the theft of the most famous portrait in the world. Perugia was outraged! He hadn't stolen the *Mona Lisa*—he had merely rescued her! What was the world coming to if the police couldn't tell the difference between theft and rescue? The rightful owners of the *Mona Lisa* were the citizens of Italy, and he, Perugia, had finally restored her to them! Was this the thanks he got?

During his four months in a jail cell, while he waited to make this pitch to a judge, Perugia had plenty of time to tell his story to the press—and each time the story got better.

Before Perugia's arrest, the police suspected everyone. Artist Pablo Picasso was arrested and interrogated, and so was poet Guillaume Apollinaire. They had both been involved in an earlier theft of two small statues from the Louvre, though Picasso always claimed he had no idea the statues were stolen.

THE JUDGMENT

An unpopular decision

The judge at Perugia's hearing seemed to be the only person in Italy who still had doubts. He sentenced Perugia to a further year and fifteen days in prison. But the resulting public uproar made an appeal judge realize that he would be enormously popular if he set Perugia free, and it was announced that Perugia would not be extradited to France. (The fact that France hadn't actually requested Perugia's extradition wasn't mentioned.) Perugia left the court a free man.

No one besides Perugia was ever arrested for the theft of the *Mona Lisa*. (The Lancelottis were apparently not important enough to charge.)

The *Mona Lisa* was returned to France via a triumphant European tour. Tens of thousands turned out, and riot police had to be brought in several times.

AT THE LOUVRE, OVER 10,000 PEOPLE LINED UP TO SEE HER IN THE FIRST TWO DAYS ALONE.

FINALLY, SHE WAS MOVED TO HER NEW, SAFER LOCATION IN THE SALLE DES ÉTATS.

SECRETS REVEALED

A very profitable plan

So who was the true mastermind of the *Mona Lisa* theft, and why did he never take possession of the priceless portrait?

It turns out that the Signore was a Paris art dealer by the name of Eduardo de Valfierno. In January 1910, Valfierno read an article in a Paris newspaper about security lapses at the Louvre—including the fact that on Mondays the entire museum was guarded by fewer than a dozen guards. This put an idea into his head.

Valfierno specialized in selling forged or stolen artwork to dishonest buyers, so he contacted a number of his very rich clients to offer them the possibility of buying the world's most famous portrait "should she become available" (*wink, wink*). The price was considerable—the equivalent of roughly $5 million today. Yet Valfierno apparently had little trouble finding six willing buyers—five of them American, one Brazilian.

Next he consulted with Yves Chaudron, perhaps the most talented art forger in the western world at that time.

Many art forgers learn to imitate an artist's techniques, studying materials, frames, paints, and brush strokes. But technology is the enemy of forgery. Even an ordinary X-ray can detect whether any alterations or repairs have been made. And while artists sometimes do reuse their own canvases, if the painting underneath is obviously more modern than the forgery on top, that's a dead giveaway!

Valfierno and Chaudron had worked together before and they trusted each other. Chaudron eventually agreed to forge six extremely high-quality copies of the *Mona Lisa*—copies so excellent, they even duplicated the chemical composition of Leonardo da Vinci's fifteenth-century paints, and imitated his exact brush strokes.

IT WAS A JOB THAT TOOK CHAUDRON WELL OVER A YEAR.

VALFIERNO SHIPPED FIVE OF THE FAKES TO A WAREHOUSE IN NEW YORK, AND THE SIXTH TO A BANK VAULT IN RIO DE JANEIRO.

After that, everything fell neatly into place. The real *Mona Lisa* was stolen on August 21, 1911. The newspaper headlines announcing her theft exploded across the world two days later. Valfierno waited a few more days to make sure all six of his customers had heard the news—then sent each man a discreet note informing him that his "purchase" was on its way. When each man received his fake, he assumed it was the stolen portrait.

Now, of course, Valfierno had no further use for the real *Mona Lisa*. It didn't matter to him whether she was found or not. Their acceptance of the fakes had made every one of his customers a criminal accessory to the real *Mona Lisa*'s theft, so none of them could risk going to the police to complain. It might have been tidier to destroy the real portrait, or to send Perugia his second payment to keep him quiet, but for some reason Valfierno did neither. Perhaps he wanted the real *Mona Lisa* restored to the world once she had filled his bank account.

Valfierno retired to Morocco, where he died a rich and free man in 1931. Chaudron retired to a quiet life on the outskirts of Paris.

And Perugia—well, Perugia never stopped complaining that he'd gotten a raw deal. But on the other hand, he was able to dine out on his story anywhere in Italy for the rest of his life.

After the famous theft, more people visited the Louvre to see the place where the famous portrait *wasn't* than had ever come to see it when it *was*. Two whole years had passed since her disappearance, and people were still laying so many flowers beneath the *Mona Lisa*'s empty wall space that they had to be cleared away twice a day.

BLOWING THE VAULT AT LAGUNA NIGUEL

When it comes to planning the perfect crime, there's no such thing as being too careful!

A QUIET NIGHT

*I*f the night guard employed by the Monarch Bay Shopping Mall in the prosperous California town of Laguna Niguel had been doing his job, he might have noticed them: four men in a 1962 Oldsmobile Super 88, slowly circling the mall's branch of the United California Bank on the night of March 17, 1972. It was almost midnight, and the only sign of life at the mall was the rapidly blinking neon "Bar" sign above the restaurant a short distance north of the bank. There were still a few cars in the restaurant's parking lot, but the guard was nowhere to be seen.

And the men in the car? Turns out they were robbers, sizing up their next big heist.

THE THIEF

A very average bank robber

Amil Alfred Dinsio, age thirty-six, from Ohio, was well known to the FBI as one of the most accomplished bank robbers in the United States. During the past two decades, he had robbed at least a dozen banks, taking more than $30 million, but he had never been convicted.

Dinsio rarely said much, especially about his robberies. And he didn't stand out in a crowd—in fact, everything about Amil Dinsio was average. Average build, average height, average weight, average looks. Dinsio considered that a real professional advantage: nothing to attract the attention of police; nothing special for witnesses to identify him by.

That night, Dinsio and his partners circled the bank again and stopped at its rear entrance, out of sight of the parking lot. In the glare of the headlights, the building looked like a big square chocolate cake with a layer of frosting across the top.

FIRST STEP:
INSPECT THE ROOF.

THE PLAN OF ATTACK
Dinsio's criminal specialty

*A*mil had his own favorite method of bank robbing. There are basically two kinds of bank robbers: the "snatch-and-grabbers" and the "vault bombers." The snatch-and-grabbers burst into a bank in broad daylight, waving guns to intimidate the employees and customers. Using speed and surprise, in just a few minutes they snatch whatever they can convince the bank's employees to hand over. Then they count on a slow police response and a fast car to make their getaway. Most bank robbers belong to this category.

The bombers, on the other hand, go after the bank's vault and its safety deposit boxes. This takes a lot of time—usually two or three days—more people, and a huge amount of technical expertise. Vault bombers do their work at night or on weekends, when the bank is closed. This enormous investment in time, money, and organization has made them an increasingly rare breed in bank-robbing circles.

Amil Dinsio was a full-time, totally committed bank vault bomber.

Up on the roof, Dinsio liked what he saw. A huge air conditioner that made it easy to stay hidden from the parking lot. Exposed and readily accessible electric wires coming in from a nearby power pole. A flat, tarred roof that looked easy to cut through.

"Bring up the tools," he called down in a low voice.

It took him only a few minutes to tap into the bank's electrical cables to power his drill and then cut a test hole in the roof, muffling the noisy drill with his jacket. With the jigsaw, Dinsio then cut out a section of roof large enough to climb through and lowered a drop-light on a cord.

As he'd suspected, there was a false ceiling just below the roof to create space for all the bank's pipes, wires, and air conditioning. And there was the top of the vault—a slab of concrete protruding just above the false ceiling. So far, so good.

Next, he climbed down to look at the vault itself. Again, it was pretty much what he'd hoped for—cement that, when he pounded on it, sounded to be about 45 centimeters (18 inches) thick. Probably reinforced with steel rods 2.5 centimeters (1 inch) thick. Nothing a few sticks of dynamite couldn't handle.

Now, where was the telephone junction box? It had to be up there somewhere. It would house the connections linking the vault alarm to the nearest police station. After several minutes of exploring, Dinsio found that, too. He recognized the brand. He'd disabled that type before. No problem.

Now Dinsio replaced the cut-out piece of roof and sealed it with roofing tar from a caulking tube. Finally he signaled the all-clear. The car, which had disappeared, returned. While one of the other men swept up the sawdust and cleared away the equipment, Dinsio stuck a small mirror into the hardening tar and aimed it at a nearby hill to the east. Starting tomorrow, and right up until they hit the bank on the weekend, one of his men would be positioned in those hills with binoculars at all times, watching the reflections from that mirror. If they changed, or the mirror disappeared, they would know that someone had discovered the break-in.

Dinsio had chosen the United California Bank in this town, Laguna Niguel, because it was located in California's Orange County, one of the most affluent areas in America. Lots of rich, retired people lived in Orange County—and rich, retired people usually kept a lot of cash, gold and silver bullion, and jewelry in their safety deposit boxes. Despite this, Dinsio had discovered that the sheriff's department had assigned only one full-time and one part-time patrol car to the area—another bonus!

For Dinsio and his crew—there were six of them altogether—the next four days would be busy, without a moment to spare. There was a lot of equipment to buy and assemble: dynamite, blasting caps, sledgehammers, a cutting torch, oxygen and propane tanks, burlap sacks, shovels, all sorts of electrical and electronic gadgetry, aerosol cans of urethane foam, walkie-talkies—the list seemed endless. But Dinsio's guys knew exactly what to do.

THE GANG

Keeping it in the family

*M*ost of the guys in Dinsio's crew were from Youngstown, Ohio—Dinsio's hometown. In fact, all but one were related to him by blood or marriage. As a rule, the more people involved in a bank robbery, the greater the chance of betrayal—but Dinsio had always found that family members were less likely to rat on each other.

Most families wouldn't have included the many kinds of experts that a vault-bombing job required, but Dinsio's family was special. It had a long history of law-breaking. Dinsio's own father, Amelio, was also a successful bank robber who, according to a newspaper report, had once run his own bank-robbing school. Most of Amil's brothers and uncles were criminals of one sort or another.

Our family picnic. "Animal" Ciasullo

"Crab" Carabbia

"Lips" Moceri

THE HEIST

A good weekend's work

To provide Dinsio's crew with a base, a relative had taken a three-month lease on a condominium a short distance from the bank. It contained a big recreation room that the crew could use as a dormitory, and as a storage and assembly shop. As part of his crew, Dinsio brought along his wife to cook and act as den mother.

Dinsio warned his crew that there were two things to worry about in this robbery. One was the Monarch Bay Drugstore, which was located right next to the bank. The bank's vault was up against the wall that the buildings shared, and the drugstore's checkout was only two paces away from the vault. No work could be done in the vault during the drugstore's hours of business. Though the bank would be closed, the Monarch Bay Drugstore stayed open all weekend. That gave Dinsio's crew only three nights to get the job done.

The second factor was the mall guard. They had already discovered that he didn't take his job very seriously, but still, two men were detailed to find out when he made his rounds, and what his routines were.

By Friday night, March 24, everything was ready to roll.

Thanks in part to the busy Dinsio clan, as well as a lot of violent mob crime, in 1963 the *Saturday Evening Post* had labeled Youngstown, Ohio, "Crimetown, USA," saying: "Officials hobnob openly with criminals. Arrests of racketeers are rare, convictions rarer still and tough sentences almost unheard of."

Minutes after the drugstore had closed and its employees had driven away, the Oldsmobile reappeared. This time, it was so weighed down with equipment that its tailpipe almost dragged on the pavement.

Now Dinsio set the ladder against the bank's rear wall again and climbed up to its outdoor alarm bell. The bell was protected by a slotted steel box that he couldn't remove. Dinsio simply poked the nozzle of a can of urethane foam through the slots and sent a surge of fast-hardening foam into the bell's clapper mechanism. Within seconds, the bell's workings were immobilized.

After fifteen minutes of listening to a scanner set up to monitor police radio transmissions, they decided that the bell hadn't triggered any alarms.

Next on the agenda was disabling the vault alarm. This would be a lot trickier. Dinsio quickly removed the piece of roof he'd cut out earlier and slid down into the bank's service area, pulling the drop-light after him. He quickly found the junction box.

DINSIO SPENT A LONG TIME STUDYING THE MAZE OF WIRES INSIDE, DECIDING WHAT TO CUT. THERE WAS NO ROOM FOR ERROR.

With each wire he cut, Dinsio got more and more nervous, while outside, the others held their breath.

Finally his head reappeared at the roof's edge. "Done," he said simply.

While two of the men carried a heavy drill rig onto the roof and wrestled it down into the service area, two more began to shovel dirt into twenty burlap sacks. Dinsio moved from place to place and man to man, keeping an eye on everything.

THEY MONITORED THE POLICE RADIO FOR HALF AN HOUR, IN CASE THE COPS WERE USING SPECIAL CODES. BUT NOBODY SHOWED UP.

LOOKS LIKE WE'RE CLEAR! LET'S MOVE!

THEY LEFT ONE MAN BEHIND TO STAY IN RADIO CONTACT WITH THE LOOKOUT ON THE HILL.

It was almost midnight before they were able to start drilling into the vault ceiling. Inside the service area, the single drop-light cast the men's long shadows eerily against the back wall. It was so bright it was hard to believe that some of the light wasn't leaking into the empty bank below, but Dinsio had checked it and found everything dark.

The sound, however, was another story. Even though they used their jackets to muffle it, there is no way to fully silence a churning concrete drill. After a few minutes, Dinsio had a brainwave: the air conditioner! He climbed down into the bank's lobby to turn it on. That helped mask the sound.

After they had drilled six finger-deep holes into the vault ceiling, they packed them with sticks of dynamite and topped them with blasting caps. Then nine of the dirt-filled sacks were packed directly over the holes to deflect the force of the blast downward. The other eleven were piled up some distance away to shield the trigger-man. When everything was ready, the trigger-man pulled on an oxygen mask and everyone else climbed out onto the roof and crouched down behind the air conditioner.

This was the most dangerous part of the whole operation.

It was just after 3:00 a.m. The restaurant was now closed and empty. The light in the guard's trailer at the other end of the mall was out, and his next security check wasn't scheduled until 6:00. Dinsio had just talked with the lookout on the hill who'd assured him that nothing looked out of the ordinary from up there.

The men behind the air conditioner looked around anxiously. Had no one noticed?

A few lights did come on in the subdivision on the other side of Monarch Bay Road, but they soon went out again. The guard's trailer stayed dark.

Dinsio listened anxiously to the police scanner.

Still nothing. No sirens, no cruisers.

The trigger-man's head popped up out of the roof hole, still masked and now heavily coated in dust and soot. He pulled off his mask.

"Better get that exhaust fan going," he said. "It's a stinker in here."

They had to run the exhaust fan for over an hour to get rid of the smoke and the stench of dynamite. Once the air had cleared enough to examine the effects of the blast, Dinsio crawled in and had a look. There was more debris than he had expected, but the blast had done the job. A ragged hole had been blown through the vault ceiling, big enough for a man to climb through. It was still crisscrossed with reinforcing rods, but a cutting torch would make short work of those.

"Looks good," Dinsio reported when he was back on the roof. "Let's haul the tanks and torches in there, and then we'll call it a night."

Half an hour later, everyone was back in the apartment, crawling into sleeping bags. Only the lookout on the hill remained at his post, keeping his binoculars trained on the bank.

They waited until 11:00 the next night before returning. This time the parking lot next to the restaurant was almost full, but the noisy bar patrons and the live band provided plenty of sound cover.

The noisiest part of the robbery was over.

Cutting away the reinforcing rods took less than an hour. By midnight, Amil Dinsio was inspecting the inside of the vault. And what he saw looked mighty promising. The vault was bursting with safety deposit boxes—over five hundred of them.

Four of the gang got to work punching out the deposit box locks with specially tapered hammers. A fifth examined the contents, quickly sifting out the valuables.

As bag after bag of treasure was passed up, the mood in the vault became giddy. One of the men began to sing. Another joined in. The jokes became raucous. This was clearly a major score!

WHEN THE SACKS WERE FULL, THEY JUST TOSSED THEM UP TO THE ROOF.

Several hours later, though, the air circulation in the tightly confined space had become so bad it was getting hard to breathe. It also became unbearably hot. The men stripped off their shirts and began to work in shifts, taking a breather on the roof every hour or so.

Even so, when dawn came and Dinsio insisted that the work stop—in case the mall guard actually showed up for his six o'clock check—the men climbed out of the vault reluctantly. There were still a few hundred safety deposit boxes to go, and it was hard to resist the temptation to carry on.

Outside, the sun was just beginning to soften the horizon above the Laguna Hills. Birds had begun to sing in the rhododendron bushes along the side of the bank. After the previous night's racket, the restaurant and bar stood closed and shuttered, seemingly abandoned. The parking lot was completely empty.

"One more night, boys," Dinsio said. "One more, and it's a wrap." He turned and waved to the invisible lookout in the hills .

Safety deposit boxes: Most banks offer their customers the opportunity to rent a safety deposit box. These small units each have their own lock, and they are stored inside the bank's vault. Often they are used to safeguard important documents, valuable jewels, or other items that customers don't need every day and want protected from home burglary. So that not just anyone can open your safety deposit box, you need to show ID, provide a signature that matches the signature card, and bring your key.

THE CLEANUP
The Devil is in the details

Most of Sunday the men felt jumpy. The mop-up of a bank robbery always took a lot longer than expected, and if the score was successful, there was always the chance you'd get too confident, too sloppy.

Back at their condominium, every piece of equipment had to be wiped down with solvent to remove fingerprints, and every article of clothing had to be washed. The walls, furniture, and even the floors had to be wiped absolutely clean. Every little piece of discarded paper, packaging, or garbage had to be removed.

Some gangs actually hired professionals who specialized in after-crime cleanup, but Dinsio didn't believe in entrusting such important work to strangers. By Sunday afternoon, he had everyone hard at work. He was so fussy and obsessive about it that he annoyed everybody.

When they returned to the bank at dusk, half the gang attacked the last of the safety deposit boxes, and the rest began to clean up. Every surface, every piece of metal or wood that anyone might have touched was scrubbed. Dinsio assigned two men to search the area around the bank to make sure nothing had been dropped or forgotten. "Take a rag and wipe out any tire marks in the dirt, too," he instructed. "One of the worst giveaways is tire marks."

When the last man had climbed out of the vault, Dinsio climbed back in to do a final double-check.

The vault looked thoroughly ransacked. The floor was knee-deep in paper debris, and the cabinets with their mangled deposit boxes looked as if they'd been hit by a bulldozer. Dinsio looked around for

BANG!
BANG!
BANG!

telltale cigarette butts, candy wrappers, toothpicks—anything that might give the police a hint. But everything looked clean.

Before climbing back out, Dinsio smashed the vault's time-lock from the inside. This would make it impossible for the bank's employees to get into the vault on Monday morning, giving the gang another half day or so before the break-in was discovered.

Back at the apartment, they transferred all the loot into packing cases to be shipped to Ohio by truck. Then everyone helped Dinsio's wife with the final wipe-down. The Oldsmobile was stored in the garage of an acquaintance until one of the local gang members could dispose of it and its contents. Everyone shook hands, and the out-of-towners headed for the airport.

It had been a trademark Dinsio heist.

Or had it?

THE DISCOVERY
The police haven't got a clue

At 8:00 Monday morning, the bank's assistant manager arrived ahead of everyone else as usual, to unlock the bank and open the vault.

The bank doors unlocked just fine, but the vault door seemed to be jammed.

The assistant manager twirled the combination dial again and again. The door wouldn't budge.

By 10:00, when even a locksmith had been unable to solve the problem, a service technician from the vault manufacturer was called. He worked on the lock until mid-afternoon before giving up.

Eventually, the technician suggested that the only option left was to drill into the vault ceiling from the service area. He led the way through a hatch in the bank's false ceiling to show the manager what he meant.

That's when the $8-million break-in of the Laguna Niguel branch of the United California Bank was finally discovered.

At the time, Dinsio's heist was the biggest bank robbery in U.S. history, but rumor has it that the gang was actually after an even bigger haul. Some people say that Dinsio chose this branch of the United California Bank because he believed—mistakenly, as it turned out—that President Richard Nixon was storing $30 million in undeclared campaign contributions in a safety deposit box there.

THE POLICE AND THE FBI WERE IMMEDIATELY NOTIFIED.

EMPLOYEES, SECURITY PERSONNEL, AND EVEN CUSTOMERS WERE INTERVIEWED.

EVIDENCE WAS EXAMINED, SORTED, AND CROSS-CHECKED.

EVERY CONCEIVABLE SURFACE WAS DUSTED FOR FINGERPRINTS.

NO LUCK!

THE FATAL ERRORS
A notable name, a big tip, and some dirty dishes

*O*ver a hundred police officers and FBI agents worked long and hard on the case for over two months without one useful result. Employees, security personnel, and even customers were interviewed. Every conceivable surface was dusted for fingerprints.

And that's where the story might have ended—except that a mere two months later, Dinsio robbed a bank in Lordstown, Ohio, using the same crew and the identical method he had used for the Laguna Niguel heist.

Being in Dinsio's home state, the Lordstown police were familiar with his methods and immediately suspected him. Although they couldn't arrest him—like the Laguna Niguel robbery, the one in Lordstown was frustratingly "clean"—they informed the FBI of their suspicions, and the FBI immediately saw the similarities. The FBI still had no hard evidence, either—but now they had a name.

They began by asking all commercial airlines flying into Los Angeles to check their records for an Amil Dinsio. To their astonishment, they hit pay dirt. For some reason, Dinsio had flown to Los Angeles on his way to Laguna Niguel under his own name!

Then they managed to find the cabbie who had taken Dinsio and his crew to their rented condominium. The cabbie remembered the place and took the police to the address. The apartment was still empty—the lease had only just ended, and a new tenant hadn't yet been found.

The police immediately searched and dusted the entire apartment. Nothing—as usual.

BUT THEN SOMEONE MADE AN INCREDIBLE DISCOVERY.

The dishwasher had been filled, but not run! It was still full of unwashed dishes! Those dishes gave the FBI an excellent collection of prints from the entire gang. Phone records of all calls made from the apartment led the police to the man in whose garage the Oldsmobile had been stored—stored and unwisely not yet disposed of. A search of the car turned up many of the gang's tools—*and* a few jewels that had dropped unnoticed out of one of the burlap sacks.

Checkmate!

It took the FBI another year to make their case legally watertight, but once they did it was game over for Dinsio and his gang. Almost all of them got twenty years in the slammer.

And the moral of the story? No job is completed until the dishes are done!

TAKE THE MONEY AND FLY

The robber and his loot dropped into the night sky ... but did he live to enjoy it?

THE HEIST
A well-planned flight

It was 4:45 on the evening of Wednesday, November 24, 1971. North-west Airlines Flight 305 had just reached cruising altitude on its short hop from Portland, Oregon, to Seattle, Washington. There were thirty-six passengers onboard, plus a three-person flight crew and two flight attendants.

The call button above seat 15D lit up, and flight attendant Florence Schaffner went to investigate. When she saw that the male passenger had a note for her, she wasn't too surprised. After all, one of the challenges of being a flight attendant was learning how to refuse requests for a date without being rude. She wasn't even going to look at it.

The man insisted. The handwritten message read: *I have a bomb in my briefcase. I will require $200,000 in $20 bills and four*

parachutes. These items must be delivered
to me at Seattle Airport as soon as we land. If these demands are
not met, I will blow up this aircraft.

Schaffner rushed nervously to the cockpit, the note flapping in
her hand.

"It's got to be a hoax," Captain William Scott said. "I'll go talk to
him."

He turned the controls over to his co-pilot, walked back to Row 15,
and sat down across the aisle. He and the hijacker spoke quietly, and at

one point, the man reached under his seat and hauled up a briefcase, opening it quickly. When Scott returned to the cockpit, his expression was grave.

"He's serious," he said. "He's got some red cylinders wired together in his briefcase that could be a bomb." For the next twenty minutes, radio messages flashed back and forth. The captain called Seattle traffic control, who called the Seattle police, who called the FBI, who called Northwest Airlines president Donald Nyrop.

What should they do? Refuse the hijacker's demands and hope that the bomb was a fake? Try to overpower the man in the air? Pretend to cooperate and then storm the plane when it landed? It was Nyrop's call.

At 5:05 p.m.—as Flight 305 began its descent toward Seattle Airport —Scott finally received a radio message from Nyrop. "Give him anything he wants."

The hijacker now informed Scott that he wouldn't allow the plane to land until the money and the parachutes were ready for pickup.

"But we're on final approach," Scott protested.

"Then abort it," the hijacker ordered.

"Be reasonable," Scott pleaded. "We haven't got a lot of extra fuel."

"You've got half an hour's worth of extra fuel," the hijacker said calmly. "Just tell the police to hurry up."

This was the FBI's first indication that this hijacker had really done his homework.

By now, they had determined that the hijacker had checked in at Portland International Airport under the name of Dan Cooper. It was also increasingly clear that he had planned his heist with impressive care. With forty-one passengers and crew in an airliner circling

THE PLANE WENT INTO A HOLDING PATTERN OVER THE AIRPORT WHILE FBI AGENTS GATHERED THE MONEY AND THE CHUTES.

above Seattle on a limited amount of fuel, the FBI had no time to mark or booby-trap the ransom money, as they normally would have. And because Cooper had demanded four parachutes, they couldn't be sabotaged—they had to assume there was a chance that some of the flight crew might be forced to use them, too.

By the time the agents had assembled the money and the parachutes, Flight 305 had been circling the airport for more than half an hour, and its tanks were almost dry.

"We're ready down here," traffic control radioed at 5:34 p.m. "Come on in."

At 5:40 p.m., Northwest Flight 305 finally landed safely at the Seattle-Tacoma Airport. Most of its passengers still had no idea that anything unusual was going on.

THE GETAWAY
Exiting a plane the hard way

Cooper ordered Scott, his flight crew, and one flight attendant to squeeze into the cockpit and shut the door. Then he let the passengers and the second flight attendant get off. As an FBI agent climbed up the ramp with the parachutes and a canvas bag filled with money, Cooper kept one hand clamped inside his briefcase. He ordered the agent to drop everything just inside the aircraft door and leave.

"Fuel up the plane," he told Captain Scott as he let everyone back out of the cockpit. "Get flight clearance for a low-altitude course from Seattle to Reno. I want you to fly no higher than 10,000 feet and no faster than 150 knots an hour. Keep your flaps and landing gear down, and the cabin unpressurized. And Captain," he added, "I'll know if my instructions aren't being followed. I'm wearing an altimeter."

It was becoming clear to Scott what Cooper had in mind: 10,000 feet (about 3,000 meters) was the highest altitude from which a parachutist could safely jump without oxygen. Once they reached 10,000 feet, Cooper ordered everyone into the cockpit and closed the door. Now the flight crew could no longer see what he was doing.

Of the commercial jets, only a Boeing 727 could fly as slow as 150 knots (250 kilometers per hour) without stalling. It also had a rear door that could be opened during flight, and that door and the jet's engines were positioned in such a way that they wouldn't endanger an exiting parachutist.

FINALLY, HE WAS READY.

Up in the cockpit, a red warning light lit up, indicating that a door had been opened during flight.

"Is everything all right back there?" Captain Scott called over the intercom. "Can we help you with anything?"

"No," Cooper called back.

That was the last word anyone heard from him.

Later, after it was discovered how Cooper had made his escape, all Boeing 727s were modified with "Cooper vanes"—a device that prevented the door on the bottom of the plane from opening during flight.

THE MANHUNT
Finding a needle in a haystack

FBI agents recovered sixty-six unidentified fingerprints on the plane, and two of the four parachutes. Anyone who had seen him in Portland, Seattle, or Reno was interrogated.

From interviews with the flight crew and passengers, the FBI quickly produced an artist's conception of what Cooper looked like. They distributed a "Wanted" poster throughout the U.S. Postal system for the hijacker.

The story ran in newspapers, on television, and on the radio—for the next several days it was headline news.

A BULLETIN FROM THE FBI

ARTIST'S CONCEPTION OF THE HIJACKER WHO EXTORTED $200,000 FROM NORTHWEST AIRLINES ON NOVEMBER 24, 1971

Due to a mix-up, an FBI spokesman mistakenly identified the hijacker as "D. B. Cooper," and that's the name by which he became known to the public. Tips, hunches, and suggestions poured into FBI offices all over the United States. Search planes flew the entire 1,000-kilometer (600-mile) route between Seattle and Reno, duplicating the airliner's flight path.

None of these efforts produced a single useful lead. D. B. Cooper—or whatever his name was—seemed to have vanished from the face of the earth.

Several days later, an idea occurred to Captain Scott. He suggested dumping a package weighing roughly the same as a man and a parachute out of the back door of a 727 in flight, to see if its sensitive flight instruments would register such a "jump." If they did, technicians could then check Flight 305's November 24 flight recorder to find out exactly when a similar jump might have happened during its Seattle-to-Reno flight. That would allow them to determine at least the general area where the vanished hijacker might have landed.

Would a man jumping out of a 69,000-kilogram (150,000-pound) airliner have made much of a difference to its flight settings? Not likely—but the FBI was getting desperate and decided to give it a try.

Sure enough, when they tried the experiment and dropped the package, the plane bobbed slightly, and its autopilot instantly trimmed back the flaps just a touch.

"We got it!" the pilot shouted.

The technicians studied the plane's flight recorder and compared the results with the records from Flight 305. What they saw was that the airliner's autopilot had trimmed back the plane's flaps in exactly the same manner on November 24, just as the plane had passed over Cowlitz and Clark counties, about 65 kilometers (40 miles) northeast of Vancouver, Washington. Calculating the direction and strength of the winds in this area for November 24 to determine the drift of Cooper's parachute, the FBI decided that the area around the town of Ariel, Washington, was most likely where Cooper had landed.

OVER 300 SOLDIERS, POLICE, FBI AGENTS, AND VOLUNTEERS SWARMED THROUGH THE FOREST.

THEY FLOATED DOWN CREEKS AND RIVERS.

AND THEY MADE RECONNAISSANCE FLIGHTS.

They were all looking, in the words of one pilot, "for a parachute or a hole." Excitement built quickly when a pilot saw what appeared to be a parachute hanging from a spruce tree, but unfortunately it turned out to be a deflated weather balloon. A large piece of orange fabric in a meadow sent expectations soaring but turned out to be a tarp-covered teepee. A number of skeletons were even discovered, but none turned out to be that of D. B. Cooper.

Finally, after eighteen days of futile searching, a heavy snowstorm brought the operation to an end.

This didn't, however, close the FBI's file on Dan Cooper. The following spring, they mounted a similar operation covering almost double the previous area, using an even larger battalion of soldiers from nearby Fort Lewis. Again, no luck. It seemed as though the investigation had reached a dead end.

Then, a full seven years later, in the fall of 1978, three hikers strolling along a logging road in Cowlitz County found the remains of an emergency door exit sign that appeared to have been sucked out of an airliner. The FBI were able to confirm that it had indeed come out of a 727. That, at least, suggested that investigators were on the right track.

One piece of evidence that later helped the FBI was Cooper's tie, which he left behind on the plane. From the tie the investigators were able, in 2001, to take a DNA sample, which allowed them to rule out a number of suspects in the case.

A YEAR LATER, 8-YEAR-OLD BRIAN INGRAM BECAME FAMOUS WHEN HE FOUND $5,800 ON THE BANKS OF THE COLUMBIA RIVER.

WHEN A THIRD BUNDLE WAS DUG UP AT THE SAME SITE, THE FBI HAD THE BILLS ANALYZED.

THE MONEY WAS FROM COOPER'S THEFT.

But since then, the trail has gone cold. Although hundreds of treasure-seekers continue to dig, no further banknotes or evidence of any other kind has ever turned up.

As of this telling, D. B. Cooper remains uncaught—the only hijacking extortionist in American history ever to successfully evade the FBI's efforts to bring him to justice. His file remains open, and his case officially unsolved.

THE ROBBER
Will the real D. B. Cooper please stand up?

So who *was* Dan Cooper, and what *did* happen to him? Did he survive his parachute jump and live to enjoy his ill-gotten gains? Was he killed on landing? Or was he wounded, and died of exposure in the wilderness?

Perhaps the most convincing explanation came in 1983, when Max Gunther, a New York journalist, received a call from a woman who gave her name as Clara.

Clara explained that she had recently lost her husband, a man she called Paul Cotton. Paul had been a great fan of Max Gunther's articles, and so it was to Gunther that she wished to offer Paul Cotton's extraordinary story.

"Just how extraordinary?" Gunther was often pestered by people who felt he simply had to tell their amazing stories to the world.

"He was Dan Cooper, the skyjacker," Clara said.

"Well, you certainly have my attention," Gunther told her. "But I'm going to be pretty hard to convince."

As Clara told her husband's story, Gunther noticed that she knew many details that had never been published, facts that the FBI had kept secret in order to test people. She knew that the name on the flight ticket had been Dan Cooper, not D. B. Cooper. She knew exactly what Cooper had been wearing that night, as well as the color of his parachute and where he had buried it. And she knew why only a small number of the stolen banknotes had been found on the banks of the Columbia River.

SECRETS REVEALED
What Clara knew

Cooper's plan, Clara said, was to land far enough out of town to avoid being seen, then bury his parachute and suit jacket. What flight attendant Schaffner had described as his "stocky build" had actually been a heavy sweater under his dress shirt. Heavy sweaters and backpacks (even when filled with banknotes) tended to pass unnoticed in logging towns. He'd spent enough time exploring the area to be sure about that sort of thing.

And according to Clara, Captain Scott's calculations were remarkably accurate. Cooper had indeed jumped out of the airliner over Clark County near the Lewis River, into a blinding rainstorm. An experienced paratrooper who had served a stint in the U.S. Army, Cooper let himself fall toward earth at a breathtaking 200 kilometers per hour (120 miles per hour), resisting the urge to pull his ripcord until his altimeter showed just over 1,000 meters (3,000 feet).

Though Clara said her husband was a paratrooper, the FBI wasn't so sure that their skyjacker was an experienced skydiver. According to one agent, "No experienced parachutist would have jumped in the pitch-black night, in the rain, with a 200-mile-an-hour wind in his face, wearing loafers and a trench coat. It was simply too risky. He also missed that his reserve chute was only for training and had been sewn shut—something a skilled skydiver would have checked."

WHEN COOPER FINALLY RELEASED HIS CHUTE, IT SLAMMED OPEN SO VIOLENTLY THAT IT WAS LIKE HITTING A MOUNTAINTOP. SECONDS LATER, HE EMERGED OUT OF HEAVY RAINCLOUDS.

DISTRACTED AND FALLING FAST, HE WAS TOO LATE TO PREPARE FOR A PROPER LANDING.

A STAB OF PAIN SHOT THROUGH HIS RIGHT ANKLE AS HE HIT THE GROUND.

HE COULDN'T SEE A THING, AND ALL HE COULD HEAR WAS THE WIND ROARING IN THE TREES AND CHURNING WATER NEARBY. NOTHING TO DO BUT TRY TO SLEEP TILL MORNING.

At dawn, the rain was still falling and the sky was a dark, glowering gray. All around him, huge cedar and hemlock trees creaked and moaned. Cooper's clothes were drenched, and his ankle felt a lot worse. He gasped as he pulled himself up to survey the situation.

His first attempt to put weight on his right foot produced such a severe flash of pain, he cried out in agony.

It took him almost an hour to find and cut himself a walking stick. Then he pulled a wad of banknotes out of the canvas bag and distributed them among his pockets. He buried the bag and the rest of the money, the chute, and the suit jacket in a shallow hole under a nearby log. By the time he was able to begin a slow hobble toward the town of Ariel, he was so exhausted with pain he was on the verge of passing out.

He didn't make it all the way to town. Near a cabin on a gravel road about 1.6 km (a mile) from Ariel's outskirts, he found a toolshed with its door unlocked. He barely managed to get inside before he lost consciousness completely.

As it turned out, that toolshed belonged to Clara's uncle. It was in the yard near his cabin, an out-of-the-way little place on the Lewis River.

Clara had always been the baby of her family, and even after she'd grown up her parents had made sure she lived a quiet life close to home. Neither her marriage nor her job as a secretary had lasted very long. While her uncle was living overseas, Clara, thirty-seven years old, was living alone in the cabin, looking after his dog, and wondering whether anything exciting was ever going to happen to her.

THE NEXT MORNING, THE DOG WAS BARKING AND WHINING AT THE DOOR OF THE TOOLSHED. CLARA WENT OUT TO INVESTIGATE.

Clara often wondered later why she didn't just call the sheriff. But there was something about this man's calm manner and his obvious helplessness that eased her fear. So instead, she helped him into her cabin and made him some tea, then drove him to a local doctor. As his broken ankle was being splinted, she introduced him as a visiting cousin.

He'd told her his name was Paul Cotton, and that he was from California, but he'd been vague about what he was doing in Washington and how he'd hurt himself. He mentioned something about bad debts, and she suspected he was on the run. But Clara didn't mind—she agreed to let him stay.

In time, he revealed a little more about himself. Childhood in Canada, teenage years in New Jersey. A stint in the U.S. Army as a paratrooper, a boring marriage, two kids. A career as a salesman, a house in the suburbs. And his eventual decision to chuck it all. Clara could easily sympathize.

SHE FOUND A STRANGER LYING ON THE FLOOR, OBVIOUSLY IN PAIN.

CLARA'S NEXT MOVE

They were watching the news on television when the FBI's drawing of D. B. Cooper flashed onto the screen. And suddenly the possibility that the man in the drawing and the man beside her were the same person hit Clara so strongly, she knew immediately that she must have suspected it for some time.

She asked him, quickly, before she lost her nerve: "Are you the hijacker? Are you D. B. Cooper?"

To her astonishment, he didn't even try to deny it.

"My lord," she said, dropping her head into her hands. "What do we do now?"

He sat unmoving on the couch where she'd settled him, his splinted leg propped up on her coffee table.

"I guess that's up to you, Clara," he said.

What happened, over the next several weeks, was that Paul and Clara fell in love. And though neither admitted it at the time, the danger they found themselves in gave their relationship an extra excitement.

Only a few weeks later, in mid-December, a wave of soldiers and FBI agents swept through the town, searching for D. B. Cooper. Everyone in the area was questioned. But by some miracle, the doctor who had splinted Paul's leg didn't make the connection. Neither did his nurse, or the few people who had seen him in Clara's car that day. Still, Paul had to hide in Clara's attic until the search party left town.

Not long after Christmas, they decided it was probably safe to dig up Paul's money. They found the parachute quickly, but after half an hour of searching the woods they'd almost given up on finding the money—when the bag, thoroughly chewed up by animals, finally turned up near the banks of a creek.

A lot of the money was missing, but, digging around in the snow, they managed to recover $96,000 in soggy, muddy bills. Together with the banknotes Paul had taken with him earlier, that made $158,000.

So now Paul and Clara were rich, but only in theory. The FBI hadn't had time to mark the bills, but they'd published their serial numbers. Trying to pass the bills would be risky. They sat around night after night, brainstorming, trying to figure out how they could possibly turn their theoretical fortune into a real one.

They decided to head for New York City. Surely in a city that big they would solve the problem. But they were startled to find that the D. B. Cooper story hadn't died.

D.B. COOPER,

WHERE ARE YOU?

IT WAS ENOUGH TO SCARE PAUL AND CLARA BACK INTO HIDING.

CASHING IN

What good is money that you can't spend?

Four years later, in 1975, the money was still locked in a suitcase in Paul and Clara's basement. They had no idea how to spend it safely, and it was beginning to look as if it might just stay there forever.

They had both found jobs, but scraping by working nine to five wasn't exactly the life they'd fantasized about in the little cabin on the Lewis River. That suitcase full of money in the basement was supposed to transform their nondescript lives into something exceptional.

And then, in 1976, Paul finally solved the problem. Casinos! A friend who'd recently returned from Las Vegas expressed surprise at the huge amounts of cash that poured through the casinos there. On his next business trip to Nevada, Paul took along a bundle of banknotes, bought $50,000 worth of chips, played for an hour, and won $500.

WHEN HE CASHED OUT, THE CASINO PAID HIM BACK IN UNIDENTIFIABLE $50 BILLS. THE SPELL ON THE MONEY WAS FINALLY BROKEN.

Paul and Clara wasted little time in getting to work on their dream. In 1976, $158,000 wasn't going to buy them palaces and yachts, but it was enough to pay for a lovely home on New York State's Long Island, in a community that welcomed them with open arms. They made friends. They joined clubs and charities. Their home became a regular gathering place for the community.

Their own relationship flourished, too. Paul romanced Clara with flowers and chocolates. They took leisurely holidays together. Was it all too good to last?

Sometimes Clara found herself wondering whether it was right to enjoy so much happiness when it had been bought with stolen money. It was the only thing she and Paul never talked about.

And then, late in 1980, a shadow fell over their lives. A personnel clerk discovered that the college degree Paul had claimed in his job application was bogus. Paul had never even been enrolled at that college.

Paul was fired. He never recovered from this blow. Without letters of reference, he couldn't find another job, despite hundreds of applications and dozens of interviews. He became moody and depressed. He'd leave the house in the morning and not come back till late at night.

The interest in D. B. Cooper never seemed to go away—it had really captured the public's imagination, inspiring a song (Thom Bresh's "D. B. Cooper, Where Are You?"), several movies, a play, and at least half a dozen books.

CLARA COULDN'T UNDERSTAND IT—UNTIL SHE DISCOVERED WHERE HE'D BEEN SPENDING HIS TIME.

"JUST WATCHING THE PLANES," HE TOLD HER.

Clara's heart sank. She asked him anxiously whether he was going to "do it again."

He didn't deny it. But he wouldn't discuss it, either.

Their life together collapsed. Clara found it impossible to eat or sleep. She saw disaster looming and she felt helpless to do anything about it.

Her fears were well founded. Three men who had tried to commit copycat hijackings had been shot. But Dan Cooper, or Paul Cotton, or whoever he was, never got the chance to attempt another hijacking. He died of a heart attack soon after his admission to Clara.

The FBI acknowledged that Clara's story was compelling and to all appearances convincing. However, they refused to accept it until she identified herself to them in person, and permitted them to question her. This she refused to do. She told Max Gunther that she mistrusted the FBI, and also feared a negative reaction from her family.

Clara retreated into silence, and the FBI continues to consider the case officially "unsolved."

THE NAPOLEON OF CRIME

Just as Napoleon loved his Josephine, this robber was captivated by a beautiful woman

Just after midnight on May 14, 1876, three men stood at the corner of Piccadilly and Old Bond Street in London, England. A low fog swirled around them, chilly and damp. At that hour, the shops, the sidewalks, and even the streets were deserted. The gas flames in the streetlamps flickered restlessly.

The three men spoke briefly, then headed down Old Bond Street. Several blocks along, one of them ducked into an angled doorway that allowed him a clear view of the street ahead. The other two stopped a few steps later in front of an art gallery. The gallery's front windows were filled with paintings of various subjects and sizes, but the two men seemed most interested in a smaller window on the gallery's second story, directly above.

After a last look in all directions, the larger of the two men clasped his hands into a stirrup and bent down. His short companion, a dapper gentleman dressed in an expensive frock coat, placed his right foot into the giant's hands and gripped his shoulders. With a single well-practiced heave, the giant hurled the little man up onto the gallery's overhanging roof, enabling him to grasp the second-story window ledge.

THE DAPPER LITTLE
THIEF POPPED
THE WINDOW OPEN
AND DISAPPEARED INSIDE.

IT WAS THE VERY
THING THE THIEF HAD BEEN
LOOKING FOR. A PORTRAIT
OF GEORGIANA,
DUCHESS OF DEVONSHIRE,
ONCE CALLED "THE MOST
EXQUISITE BEAUTY THAT
EVER GRACED A CANVAS."
HE STARED, TRANSFIXED.

After a while, the thief realized he was listening to the steady, rhythmic snoring of a night watchman downstairs who was supposed to be guarding this treasure.

There was no time to waste. From his coat he pulled out a sharp knife and a small pot of paste. Lifting the portrait off the wall, he carefully cut the canvas out of its frame, then smeared the paste evenly across its back to make it more flexible. Then he rolled it up very carefully with the painted side outwards, to avoid cracking the surface, and slipped it inside his coat.

After leaning out the window and giving a low whistle, he scrambled off the roof and fell into the waiting arms of his giant assistant. The third man suddenly appeared out of his doorway.

ALL IN A DAY'S WORK
FOR THE THREE THIEVES.

THE THEFT DISCOVERED
A painting that made it into the headlines ... twice!

News of the theft of the *Duchess* caused a huge uproar, both in the world of art and that of crime. The portrait, by the great English painter Thomas Gainsborough, had recently been bought by the gallery for over ten thousand pounds sterling, the highest price ever paid for a painting. The purchase had made headlines all over the western world.

The Duchess of Devonshire was a scandalous character, outraging proper English society with her reputation for decadence and questionable morals. Though Gainsborough's painting had been lost for decades—it disappeared around the same time that her husband suspected the Duchess of an affair with another man—when it at last resurfaced, it, too, caused a sensation. People lined up and bought tickets to see it, and women tried desperately to imitate her provocative look.

Scotland Yard, Britain's national police headquarters, immediately sent its agents scurrying all over England, trying to pick up the missing portrait's trail. When the agents returned empty-handed, circulars and photos of the painting were sent to police forces all over the world. Advertisements were placed in many European newspapers and magazines, and a huge reward was offered for the painting's safe return. The Pinkerton Agency, America's largest private detective agency, was engaged to investigate rumors that the painting might have been stolen for one of America's steel or oil barons. Many of them had large art collections.

THE ROBBER
A remarkable talent for crime

In fact, the man who had stolen the Gainsborough portrait was Adam Worth. In the criminal underworld, Worth was known as "The Napoleon of Crime," for both his success and his short stature. He had recently moved his criminal operations from America to England, where he had bought a racing stable, a large steam yacht, and a stately mansion in London's Piccadilly. There he entertained many of the bankers and barons he regularly fleeced.

As crooks went, Worth was definitely a cut above average. He was charming and gracious. He was disciplined, loyal, and a workaholic. He didn't drink, fight, or boast. And he was generous to a fault. Anyone working for Adam Worth knew that the boss would spend his last nickel to help him out.

Worth was the son of a German tailor who emigrated to the United States in 1849, when Worth was just five years old. Watching their parents struggling to scrape together a living apparently convinced all three of the couple's children—Adam, a younger brother John, and a sister named Harriet—that trying to make an honest living in 1840s America was hopeless. Ashamed of their poverty and impatient for the good life that the family had emigrated for, all three joined the world of crime—the two boys as thieves, and the daughter as the wife of a dishonest lawyer. Only Adam turned out to have a real knack for it.

By the time Worth stole the *Duchess*, he had been a professional thief for almost twenty years. He had stolen jewels, banknotes, and other valuables worth millions, but he had never once been convicted of a criminal offense. Both Scotland Yard and the Pinkerton Agency had tried to outwit him, but Worth had always been too clever.

Now, something quite unexpected happened.

Adam Worth, a man who had always kept control of his emotions and had never cared a fig about art (except for its value as loot), became utterly fascinated by the *Duchess*. As he studied the portrait during the days after the theft, he became so drawn to her that he decided to keep her.

This did not please his two partners in crime.

BUT THE PAINTING HAS NEVER BEEN MORE VALUABLE—EVERYONE'S TALKING ABOUT IT!

TO ME, IT'S PRICELESS. I'LL NEVER GIVE HER UP!

WORTH DID EVENTUALLY PAY THE TWO MEN THEIR SHARES, BUT THE PARTNERSHIP BROKE UP IN ANGER, WITH THE TWO MEN VOWING REVENGE.

THE OBSESSION
Memory of a lost love

As he continued to rob banks and steal millions, Worth's infatuation with the *Duchess* continued to grow. It wasn't long before just gazing at her now and then, in the secret little gallery he had built for her in his London mansion, wasn't enough.

He had a special false-bottomed trunk constructed so he could take her along on his many voyages. He even had a false-bottomed briefcase made, so that, as he went about his business, she was rarely more than an arm's length away. At night, in hotel rooms, he took her out and set her up on a table or counter so he could gaze on her to his heart's content.

As rumors about Worth and the *Duchess* began to spread through the underworld, friends suspected that his infatuation stemmed from the fact that the *Duchess* looked surprisingly like Kitty Flynn, an Irish barmaid who'd had a long affair with Worth in the early 1870s.

IN THE END, KITTY LEFT WORTH FOR A RICH CUBAN PLAYBOY. HIS FRIENDS SAID IT WAS A BLOW THAT HE NEVER RECOVERED FROM.

THE DETECTIVE
He always got his man

*O*ne man who found the rumors about Adam Worth and the *Duchess* extremely intriguing was William Pinkerton of the Pinkerton Detective Agency. Nicknamed "The Eye," Pinkerton was a world-famous detective, street-smart and ruthless. He had caught and brought to justice more famous crooks—including Jesse James and Butch Cassidy—than any other man alive. He had every intention of adding Adam Worth to his list.

The Pinkerton Detective Agency, founded by William Pinkerton's father, Allan, was at one time the largest private law enforcement organization in the world. The agency rose to fame when it provided security for President Abraham Lincoln and foiled (or so it claimed) an assassination attempt. The company, whose motto was "We Never Sleep," is still operating today.

The two men had met socially and, to everyone's surprise, liked each other immediately. Pinkerton found Worth to be smart, resourceful, and courageous. He also liked the fact that Worth never used a gun when committing his crimes. Worth, for his part, admired Pinkerton's brilliant detective work, his determination, and the fact that he always fought fair.

Whenever they met, in London, Paris, or New York, they bought each other drinks and spent an hour or two chatting. At the same time, there was never any doubt in either man's mind about what was going on. Pinkerton was determined to put Worth in jail, and Worth was determined not to let Pinkerton succeed.

Mere months after the theft of the *Duchess*, Pinkerton's spies had already reported underworld rumors linking the theft to Adam Worth. Then, almost a year later, Little Joe Elliott, one of Worth's two former partners, was arrested in New York for forging checks. Hoping to reduce his prison sentence, Elliott met with Pinkerton and betrayed Worth, providing all the details. A few months later, the other partner, giant Jack "Junka" Phillips, gave a similar story to Scotland Yard.

It was only hearsay evidence—not enough for an arrest. But when an embarrassed Scotland Yard finally appealed to the Pinkerton Agency for help, Pinkerton agreed. During his next trip to the United States, Pinkerton's detectives raided Worth's hotel, looking for the thief and the painting. But Worth had checked out only hours before.

WORTH ALMOST RAN INTO THE ARMS OF TWO DETECTIVES. BUT HE WAS SLIPPERY AND MADE HIS ESCAPE—WITH THE *DUCHESS*.

Days later, Pinkerton's men tracked Worth to another fancy hotel in Buffalo, New York, where he was having dinner with his sister and brother-in-law.

Worth hastily took the next train out of town, and for the remainder of his travels in America he kept the *Duchess* safely hidden in a Boston warehouse.

But if Worth had expected to find peace and tranquility on his return to London, he was mistaken. Instead, he found that his mansion had been raided and a Scotland Yard detective permanently stationed out front! Clearly, it was time to take a very long holiday.

Worth spent the next several years traveling throughout the Middle East, Europe, and South Africa. He robbed mail trains, hijacked diamond shipments, fleeced banks, and raided safety deposit boxes. He swindled investment houses, stole bonds, faked insurance claims, and blew up safes. Often the *Duchess* would be left in a warehouse, but whenever he felt it was safe he took the painting with him—not hidden in a trunk or briefcase, but rolled up and tucked into the inside pocket of his overcoat.

As the years went by and Worth managed to evade every effort by both William Pinkerton and Scotland Yard to recover the *Duchess*, the heat finally did die down. Worth returned to his London mansion, his racing stable, and his thoroughbreds. Scotland Yard eventually withdrew the lookout in front of his house. Worth became the mentor for a whole new generation of criminals. He even got married, and had a son and daughter.

But through it all—despite threats from Scotland Yard, blackmail attempts by other criminals, and even enticing offers from insurance companies—he still refused to give up the *Duchess*.

THE BEGINNING OF THE END
Napoleon meets his Waterloo

And then, in 1892, sixteen years after the theft, Adam Worth made the mistake that every police force in the western world had been hoping for.

It had all started in February 1884 with the news that an old friend and partner, Charley Bullard, had been caught trying to rob a bank in Liège, Belgium. Bullard was sentenced to twelve years' hard labor in the Prison de Louvain. Prisons in Belgium were notorious for their brutality, and more than five years was considered a death sentence—few inmates were able to survive longer than that.

For the next eight years, Adam Worth tried everything he could think of to free his old partner. He paid bribes. He hired expensive lawyers. He petitioned politicians with clemency requests. Nothing worked.

Finally, in 1892, Worth decided to travel to Belgium himself, possibly hoping to coordinate a prison break to free Bullard. When he arrived in Liège, he discovered Charley Bullard had died.

The news hit Worth hard. He spent the next several days just walking around Liège, mourning the loss of his old friend.

Charley Bullard—also known as "Piano Charley"—was a gifted musician as well as a notorious and talented safecracker. Worth had already helped Bullard escape from prison once, in 1869, by tunneling into his friend's cell and bribing two guards to keep quiet.

As he wandered the streets, though, something caught Worth's attention. He couldn't help noticing that the armored express van that made daily currency deliveries to the city's banks was guarded only by a single armed driver and an unarmed apprentice. Intrigued, Worth followed the van. He saw that occasionally, when they had packages for several adjacent buildings, the two men made their deliveries simultaneously, leaving the van briefly unguarded.

Putting aside his grief for a moment, Worth considered the potential profit and deemed it an opportunity too good to waste. Charley Bullard would have understood.

Worth called in Johnny Curtin, an American bank robber hiding out in London, and "Dutch Alonzo" Henne, a London mobster, to join him.

Worth would arrange to have a delivery made to an office close to a downtown bank. The driver would presumably make the bank delivery, while the apprentice delivered Worth's bogus package. As soon as the van was unattended, Worth would slip inside, smash the

9:30 A.M. TWO DELIVERIES: ONE TO THE BANK, THE OTHER WORTH'S BOGUS PACKAGE.

WORTH WORKED QUICKLY TO EMPTY THE STRONGBOX.

BUT WHERE WAS CURTIN?

lock off its strongbox, grab the contents, and hand them off to Curtin, who would be passing by pretending to be an innocent tourist. Big Dutch Alonzo would stay nearby to apply some muscle if anything went wrong.

Simple, quick, and easy. But that wasn't how it played out.

Instead of taking the handoff from Worth, Curtin was running as fast as he could in the opposite direction, while Alonzo similarly made himself scarce.

What in tarnation was going on?

There was no time to speculate. Clutching the bag, Worth jumped out of the van and began to hurry away himself.

"Stop thief! Stop thief!" someone shouted.

Worth looked in the direction of the voice. A man in a railway uniform was pointing at him excitedly. "Stop him!"

At this point, the returning van driver caught sight of Worth and gave chase. So did the man in the railway uniform. The three men raced down the boulevard, Adam Worth drawing steadily ahead. For a few moments, it looked as if Worth would be able to outrace his pursuers. But at the rue Saint-Veronique, a young police patrolman heard the shouts and sprang into action.

A block later, Worth could hear the patrolman's footsteps pounding away a short distance behind. In desperation, he flung his bag into a nearby alley and tried to dodge into the shopping crowds. Too late! He was tackled by several citizens and went down. The young policeman leaped on top of him and clapped him into handcuffs.

It was game over for Adam Worth.

Or was it?

Worth told the police his name was Edward Grey. Then, despite days of interrogation, he refused to say anything more—he even refused to rat on his double-crossing accomplices.

Frustrated, the Belgian police sent Worth's photograph and description to police forces all over Europe and North America. A chorus of replies informed them that they had succeeded in catching Adam Worth, one of the greatest robbers of all time.

The court now confidently charged Adam Worth with the carefully orchestrated robbery of an official Belgian armored delivery van. After several days of testimony, the jury took only minutes to agree. Worth was sentenced to seven years of solitary confinement with hard labor in the Prison de Louvain, the prison where Charley Bullard had died.

It wasn't long before Worth sank into a deep depression. Then he developed bronchitis. The prison doctor treated this with a crude surgical operation on the inside of Worth's nose, which led to frequent, violent nosebleeds and crippling headaches.

As news of Worth's condition spread, he began to receive offers from lawyers, politicians, and even police representatives to hand over the *Duchess* in return for a shortened prison sentence. But Worth refused.

Why did Curtin and Alonzo run off and leave Worth (literally) holding the bag? People have long wondered whether these two were somehow in league with Worth's former partners, Little Joe Elliott and Jack "Junka" Phillips, who never forgave Worth for refusing to sell the *Duchess* and had sworn revenge on him.

THEN WORTH DISCOVERED THE FULL EXTENT OF JOHNNY CURTIN'S BETRAYAL.

LET ME WORRY ABOUT YOUR FINANCES. I PROMISED ADAM I'D HELP...

CURTIN CONVINCED WORTH'S WIFE TO SIGN OVER ALL OF WORTH'S WEALTH AND POSSESSIONS TO HIM.

THEN CURTIN SOLD EVERYTHING, LEAVING WORTH'S WIFE PENNILESS. SHORTLY AFTERWARD, HE DISAPPEARED. BUT STILL, WORTH REFUSED TO REVEAL WHERE HE HAD HIDDEN THE *DUCHESS.*

LAST REQUESTS
Trying to put things right

Worth was now at rock bottom. His wife was insane, the love of his life was dead, his horses, houses, yacht, and reputation were gone, his health ruined. All he had left was the *Duchess*, wrapped in a cocoon of pure silk in the warehouse where he had hidden her before heading for Belgium.

When the Belgian prison authorities finally released Adam Worth in 1897, two years early for good behavior, the Napoleon of Crime was a broken man. He was dying of tuberculosis, and filled with regret. He decided the only thing left to do was to try to provide some security for his son and daughter.

He headed to America.

A YEAR LATER, WORTH LEARNED THAT KITTY FLYNN, THE GREAT LOVE OF HIS LIFE, HAD DIED IN NEW YORK. NOT LONG AFTER, HE WAS INFORMED THAT HIS WIFE HAD GONE MAD AND, BEING PENNILESS, HAD BEEN SENT TO A LUNATIC ASYLUM.

And so, unsurprisingly, it wasn't long before William Pinkerton received a letter at home from Adam Worth, who wished to inform Pinkerton that he was finally prepared to open negotiations for the return of the *Duchess*.

The two men met in Pinkerton's office two days later. It was a meeting of historic importance for both: the western world's most famous thief and the western world's most famous detective, both having spent almost a lifetime trying to outwit each other. Worth was a wanted man in America; Pinkerton could have arrested him on the spot. But they were past that now. Their battle was over.

Worth opened negotiations by demanding $25,000 in cash, plus immunity from prosecution. He promised that the money would only be used for the support and education of his children. Pinkerton agreed, but insisted that the deal had to be handled in such a way that he—the American symbol of justice and crime-busting—couldn't be seen as an accomplice to a crime.

So the two men cooked up a story in which the relentless William Pinkerton, after years of heroic effort, had finally tracked down the famous *Duchess* to an undisclosed location in the American Midwest. But the current holder of the painting turned out not to be the thief. The current holder had been given the painting by a man—presumably the actual thief—shortly before the thief had died. So the true thief was dead, and the current holder was now claiming the posted reward for the painting's return.

The newspapers of the day bought the story completely.

For William Pinkerton, the return of the *Duchess* became his career's crowning glory and his greatest accomplishment. Adam Worth, on the other hand, could now face his imminent death with peace of mind. Pinkerton had promised to keep an eye on his children and to ensure that they were not cheated out of their support money.

Pinkerton kept his promise. When Worth died on January 8, 1902, in Camden, England, his children were with him, safe and secure. In fact, due in large part to Pinkerton's efforts, they weren't even aware that their father had been a famous thief.

Pinkerton kept an eye on Worth's children for many years after their father's death. He gave them fatherly advice, which they may have heeded, because neither of them followed in their father's footsteps.

The daughter, by some accounts, looked surprisingly like the *Duchess* at an early age. And the son—in this story's most ironic twist—eventually joined the Pinkerton Agency and became one of its most accomplished detectives !

Many people are convinced that Arthur Conan Doyle's fictional character James Moriarty, the nemesis of the great Sherlock Holmes, was actually based on the methods and exploits of Adam Worth.

BANKNOTES FROM HEAVEN

**For these thieves the robbery was the easy part ...
it was the getaway that nearly killed them!**

On July 19, 1949, at 2:50 p.m.—just before closing time—two bandits entered the Imperial Bank of Canada in the prosperous little gold-mining town of Larder Lake in northern Ontario. The bandits, wearing ordinary work clothes, each carried a suitcase with some tools and a revolver inside. Normally, they would have hidden their revolvers in their jackets, but it was roasting in Larder Lake that summer—too hot for jackets. It was also buzzing with deerflies.

The bank was one of half a dozen two-storied, false-fronted businesses lining Larder Lake's muddy main street. A row of mostly black automobiles stood parked right up against the buildings—Larder Lake had no patience for city-slicker features like sidewalks.

THE THIEVES

Looking to rob greener pastures

The bandits—Victor Desmarais and Leo Martial—hailed from Montreal. So, why were they in hot, buggy Larder Lake?

In 1906, Larder Lake had seen Ontario's first major gold rush. Four thousand prospectors had come from all over the world to try their luck there. So Desmarais and Martial decided to give the town a try. Where there was lots of gold, there was bound to be lots of cash.

Larder Lake had only one bank—one-stop shopping. They could travel to Larder Lake by train, then fly out with their loot by chartered floatplane. The setup couldn't have been more perfect.

Besides, there was too much competition in Montreal, Canada's bank robbery capital.

SORRY GUYS! THIS ONE IS EMPTY.

!?

BANK OF MONTREAL

$

IT WAS A GOOD TIME TO GET OUT OF TOWN. IN THE 1940S, MONTREAL BANKS WERE BEING KNOCKED OVER AT A RATE OF ONE EVERY 93 MINUTES!

THE HEIST
Like taking candy from a baby

"Where's the manager?" Martial demanded.

The tellers didn't know. Manager Albert Gary often spent time away from his desk without explaining where he was going.

Desmarais looked annoyed. He asked them whether either of them knew the combination to the vault. They didn't.

Desmarais decided they'd have to drill into the vault. There wasn't time to wait until the manager got back.

"The vault's open," the first teller said.

"Wouldn't he come back before closing time?" Martial asked.

"The vault's open," the teller repeated. "It's never locked during the day."

The bandits were astounded. They quickly herded both tellers to the back of the bank where the vault was located. It was true.

Desmarais and Martial couldn't believe their luck. This never would have happened back in Montreal. Was this really how people did business in the boonies? They might as well have hung a "Help Yourself" sign on it!

Desmarais kept guard over the tellers while Martial quickly stuffed all the money he could find in the vault—about $15,000—into their two suitcases.

Just then, the bell over the front door jangled. "Front door's not locked yet," one of the tellers said. He moved around a corner and looked. "Gerry Hamson," he said. "He's a mining inspector."

THE GETAWAY

Desmarais ordered the teller to call up Toni Gervanni and get him to come to the back of the bank to pick up a parcel. Martial hauled the two suitcases to the back door.

When the taxi arrived five minutes later, the three hostages were securely locked in the vault and the bandits were waiting outside the bank, suitcases bulging.

"Take us to the seaplane base," Desmarais said. "Leavern Brothers Air Service." It was twenty-eight kilometers (eighteen miles) out of town.

BY 3:45 THEY WERE AT THE FLOATPLANE BASE.

Gervanni explained that he had to pick up a parcel first. The bandits wrenched open the car's rear doors, flung in their suitcases, and slid in after them.

The bandits had ordered a seaplane to fly them out to Val-D'or, in northern Quebec. From there they could catch a commercial flight south to Montreal.

They told Gervanni to wait while they checked the arrangements with the floatplane service. Bush pilot Jack Lamont was already there, peering curiously through the front window of the office as they drove up. After a short discussion, Desmarais waved Gervanni away. The frightened taxi driver drove off in a spray of gravel.

What happened next is unclear. Some claim that Jack Lamont had caught sight of Desmarais's revolver as he climbed out of the taxi, and so the fact that his floatplane wouldn't start was actually a trick. Some say Lamont just got lucky. Whatever the case, when the pilot tried to start his single-engine Aeronca, with the bandits and their loot onboard, the motor churned but wouldn't catch. Lamont fussed with the settings and adjusted the throttle, but nothing worked.

Finally the bandits lost patience.

"Haven't you guys got another plane?" Martial demanded.

Lamont shook his head. He said he couldn't figure out what was wrong; the plane had worked just fine yesterday. He offered to phone around to see if any of the owners of the other floatplanes moored at the base might be willing to take over the job. He disappeared into his office to start phoning.

After a further ten minutes, the bandits became alarmed. Lamont seemed to be spending an awfully long time on the phone. Desmarais started checking out other planes tied to the dock and found one with its keys dangling in the ignition.

"Get that pilot!" he shouted to Martial. "He can fly us out with this one."

Martial ran off to bring back the pilot, but returned almost immediately to report that Lamont had disappeared. There was no one in the office.

Desmarais swore a volley of oaths. He had let Gervanni drive off because he'd expected to be in the air minutes later. By now, the taxi driver would have alerted the police.

Their only hope was that plane.

Although neither man was a pilot, both had flown in floatplanes before. They had also watched Lamont trying to start his Aeronca. It wasn't much, but it was their only chance. There was no more time to lose.

They hauled their suitcases into the new plane, threw off the tie lines, and leaped inside.

Desmarais searched frantically for the rudder. Once he found it, it didn't take him long to figure out how it worked. The plane straightened sharply and headed out into the lake.

Desmarais shouted something that sounded like "Hold on!" and pulled the throttle out as far as it would go. The engine howl turned into a roar and the plane sped up quickly. Now they were leaving a rooster tail of foam in their wake. They plowed across the lake at full power, all the way to the other side—but the plane wouldn't lift off. They turned around and tried it again in the opposite direction. Still no luck.

An airplane's throttle controls the flow of fuel or power to the engine. The rudder moves the nose of the plane to the left or to the right. The stick (or yoke) controls the plane's altitude.

Toni Gervanni and Jack Lamont had indeed both called Ralph Paul (whose rather grand title of "police chief" hid the fact that he was actually Larder Lake's only policeman). The hostages had been found and freed, and word of the robbery had spread through the town like wildfire. Half the town was now standing on the shore, yelling and waving, cheering and booing, watching the plane buzzing frantically back and forth across the water like a berserk mosquito. Larder Lake hadn't had so much excitement in years!

Ralph Paul had quickly called up the only policeman in nearby Virginiatown, Constable Lloyd Westlake, and the two men were assembling a posse of townspeople to give chase.

FINALLY, DESMARAIS TRIED PULLING BACK ON THE STICK, AND THAT DID IT!

HE TRIED TO TURN THE PLANE AROUND, UNSUCCESSFULLY.

THE SUITCASES FULL OF CASH TUMBLED OUT AND POPPED OPEN ...

BOOM!

... AND MONEY RAINED ALL OVER LARDER LAKE.

The sudden windfall startled several trappers who were working their trap lines near the lake that day, and thrilled the town residents, who came scrambling over from the floatplane base. Some of the money was gathered up by the posse, and some was turned in by onlookers, but some was never recovered. As one Larder Lake resident put it wryly, payday came early for some of Larder Lake's citizens that day.

Miraculously, the plane didn't catch fire when it finally smacked down in a patch of dense underbrush a short distance from the base.

The two bandits survived the crash with only cuts and bruises. They promptly disappeared into the bush, with Ralph Paul's posse—by then numbering over a hundred men—in hot pursuit.

Leo Martial didn't get very far. He was captured just over an hour later, at gunpoint, on Highway 66. He had followed a trap line that seemed to be headed away from town, but its direction had changed and he hadn't noticed. He ran right into the arms of some of Ralph Paul's volunteers who had been searching the bush around the lakeshore.

Victor Desmarais, however, managed to avoid capture until about 1:30 the next morning. He stayed clear of the trails, working his way deeper and deeper into the bush. Whether he eventually became lost or whether he decided to jump a passing freight train is unclear, but by morning he had returned to the rail line that ran along the edge of town. He was finally caught and arrested in the vicinity of the Larder Lake station, where two small boys saw him and reported him to the posse. He was hungry, badly fly-bitten, and totally exhausted.

THE VERDICT
No extra prison time for stupidity

Justice in the 1940s was handed out a lot more quickly than it is today. A mere two weeks later, both robbers had been arraigned, tried, and sentenced, and were already on their way to the nearest prison, Kingston Penitentiary. Charged with illegal confinement, possession of a prohibited weapon, and armed robbery, they had been sentenced to seven years each.

The feeling around Larder Lake was that if they'd also been charged with the gross stupidity of their getaway attempt, the length of their sentences might have been much greater.

Meanwhile, the Larder Lake robbery brought the area a degree of notoriety it could well have done without. Just over a decade later, Larder Lake Station became the target of another major heist, this one a load of gold bullion being transferred to Toronto from the surrounding gold mines. Station Master Tom Jonkin was left bound to a chair, while robbers escaped with three gold bars valued at $35,000.

Once again a plane was used, but this time it was operated by a real pilot. The robbers in this caper were never caught.

THE CLASSIEST THIEF IN MANHATTAN

When the thief is elegant, charming, and very choosy about his "clients," it might almost be a pleasure to be robbed!

LUXURY LIVING
A very expensive address

In the 1920s, New York's most luxurious hotel was, without doubt, The Plaza, located on the corner of Fifth Avenue and Central Park South. The hotel was a home away from home for many of the world's most rich and famous. The great comedian Charlie Chaplin stayed at The Plaza when he was in town. So did novelist F. Scott Fitzgerald. Presidents and kings booked suites months in advance.

Some patrons even maintained permanent apartments there, like the fabulously wealthy Woolworth department store heiress Mrs. Jessie Woolworth Donahue and her stockbroker husband James P. Donahue.

THE HEIST
A daring daylight robbery!

On September 29, 1925, the Donahues arrived at The Plaza to spend a week in New York—Mr. Donahue to see to some business matters and Mrs. Donahue to be fitted with some of the costliest pearl necklaces ever produced by Cartier of Paris. As was usual in those days, the New York newspapers reported the Donahues' arrival and the reason for their stay in the society pages.

It was an announcement Jessie Donahue would live to regret.

TWO DAYS AFTER THE DONAHUES CHECKED IN, A DISTINGUISHED-LOOKING VISITOR ARRIVED AT THE PLAZA.

The man made his way confidently through the hotel's ornate lobby and headed for the elevator cage. "Fifth floor, my good man," he told the operator.

The elevator operator bowed slightly and closed the cage gate. "Fifth floor," he repeated obediently. The cage rose silently up the shaft and stopped, gently, five floors up.

"Welcome to The Plaza, sir," the operator said, bowing again. The gate slid back on well-oiled rails.

The man in the top hat waited until the elevator cage had disappeared back down the shaft. Then he headed along the richly carpeted corridor to the emergency stairway. Looking around to make sure the corridor was empty, he slipped into the stairway and climbed up to the sixth floor. There, too, the hallway was deserted.

The Donahue apartment was only a short distance away. As he approached it, the man in the top hat drew a pair of gray silk gloves from his inside breast pocket and pulled them on. At the door, he listened intently, while watching the corridor in both directions. Then he slid a hotel pass key into the lock, and pushed open the door.

The Plaza Hotel has provided the location for more than a dozen films, including *Sleepless in Seattle*, *Home Alone 2: Lost in New York*, and *Bride Wars*. Of course, The Plaza is famously home to author Kay Thompson's beloved children's book heroine Eloise, who lives "on the tippy-top floor" with her dog Weenie, her turtle Skipperdee, and her beloved Nanny.

The master bedroom was in the middle. He knew that it had an extra-large bathroom attached to it, with its own dressing room. That's where the voices seemed to be coming from.

He moved silently across the vast expanse of the living room and listened again at the bedroom door. He eased the door open just enough to insert his head. Just as he'd thought. The door between the master bedroom and its bathroom was closed. The voices were coming from behind that door.

Taking a deep breath, he slipped into the room and quickly checked the dressing table, a large wardrobe, the luggage. Nothing. Perhaps the bureau? In the third drawer he found a heavy, velvet jewel box. This looked promising.

FINALLY, AT THE VERY BACK OF THE DRAWER, HE FOUND THEM. FIVE STRINGS OF PEARLS BY CARTIER. IF THEY WERE REAL, THEY WERE PROBABLY WORTH HALF A MILLION DOLLARS APIECE.

Inside was a large selection of pendants, brooches, and earrings. Jessie Donahue's main collection, by the look of it. The lady certainly had expensive tastes. He prodded the jewels gently, letting the light from the window sparkle through them.

Under a layer of linens he found more treasure—necklaces, a tiara, bracelets, chains. All high-quality. But they weren't what he was looking for.

He picked up a string and rubbed its center pearl slowly across his teeth. Back and forth. It was slippery. A fake. Not surprising—when rich socialites ordered jewelry, they often ordered identical-looking fake sets as well, to wear in social situations where the jewels were likely to be lost or stolen.

A burst of laughter from behind the bathroom door made him stiffen briefly. Footsteps approached. His hands hovered over the pearls, ready to grab.

The footsteps stopped at the door. A metallic clank suggested that something on a hanger had been hung on a hook.

Eyes still riveted on the door, the man in the top hat slid the next string into his mouth. Another fake.

The third and fourth strings had a gritty feel against his teeth— they were the real McCoy. He dropped them both into his pocket.

The fifth string was another fake—it was time to go.

With a few practiced flicks of his hands, he straightened the linens, replaced the case, and silently closed the last drawer. Seconds later, he was back out in the corridor.

As he hurried down the stairs to the fifth floor he stripped off his gloves. At the fifth floor he rode the elevator down to the lobby, nodded pleasantly to a bowing bell captain, and tipped his hat at the front door to an elderly lady while the doorman summoned a cab. He rode the cab for a dozen blocks, got out, hailed a cab in the opposite direction, and gave the driver an Upper West Side address.

AFTER THE CAB DROPPED HIM OFF, HE WALKED SEVERAL MORE BLOCKS, TO WHERE HE REALLY LIVED. NOW HE COULD FINALLY RELAX.

THE SEARCH IS ON

The headline on the front page of the next day's *New York Times* trumpeted: WOOLWORTH HEIRESS ROBBED AT THE PLAZA OF $750,000 IN GEMS! THIEF ESCAPES LEAVING NO CLUE.

The report explained that the robbery—one of the biggest on record—included several recently purchased strings of pearls that, alone, had been insured for a million dollars. All the more astonishing was the fact that the theft had occurred while Mrs. Jessie Donahue was in her nearby bathroom, with a maid and a masseuse in attendance the entire time.

Though Jessie's father, Frank W. Woolworth, made a fortune by creating the Woolworth's department store chain, life was not as happy for those who inherited his fortune. His daughter Edna committed suicide when her own daughter, Barbara, was only five years old. Known as the "poor little rich girl," Barbara was raised by a string of relatives and governesses, married seven times, and died nearly penniless.

Descriptions of the gems, provided by Cartier of Paris, were immediately broadcast all over the United States and to gem centers in London, Paris, Amsterdam, and Johannesburg. When New York police detectives were unable to come up with a single clue, the Donahues hired the world-famous Pinkerton Agency to solve the crime.

Neither the police nor the Pinkertons had any luck. The crime remains officially "unsolved" to this day.

THE ROBBER

When only the best will do

Though he had no intention of telling the police, years later the thief himself privately took credit for the heist. His name was Arthur Barry, arguably the greatest jewel thief in American criminal history. Barry belonged to a class of criminals known in the trade as "second-story men" or "cat burglars"—thieves who stealthily broke into the second-story bedrooms of the rich to steal their jewelry.

Second-story men considered themselves the kings of thieves. They were often every bit as snobbish as their victims. Barry, for example, only robbed people who were listed in New York's Social Register—a sort of phone book of the wealthy, which he had memorized. Being robbed by Barry soon became a sign of high social status. He referred to his victims as his "clients," and he stole only jewels, no matter what else he found.

Always elegant in his working uniform—a tuxedo and gleaming patent-leather shoes—Barry had impeccable manners, and his knowledge of art and culture was impressive.

Known as a man of independent means, he was often invited to lavish parties, where he mingled with many of his future "clients," the owners of the huge mansions on Long Island that were his favorite hunting grounds. A 1956 article about him in *Life* magazine claimed that he was so good-looking and charming that "wealthy matrons, awakening at night to find him prowling about their bedrooms, often failed to scream."

A CHANGE OF PLAN
Sometimes it pays to be flexible

Barry was both resourceful and ingenious. One afternoon, after watching the home of a rich Connecticut industrialist for several weeks and memorizing everyone's routines and schedules, Barry felt ready to pounce. But when he returned to the home that evening, he found that a family member had become seriously ill, the entire house was lit up, and there were relatives and nurses everywhere. He could see it was hopeless.

He knew, however, that the home of Percy Rockefeller was nearby, and he thought he'd have a quick look at it, instead. The Rockefellers were one of America's wealthiest families, and Percy Rockefeller was very prominent in the Social Register.

As expected, the place was enormous, with multiple turrets and chimneys and a high stone wall surrounding the entire estate. More to the point, Barry spotted two bull mastiffs patrolling the lawns—guard dogs probably trained not to accept food from strangers, and to attack at the slightest provocation.

BARRY RETURNED THE NEXT AFTERNOON, DRESSED AS A TELEPHONE LINEMAN, AND DISCONNECTED THE BURGLAR ALARM THAT WOULD HAVE ALERTED THE POLICE.

BARRY FOUND A KENNEL WILLING TO SELL HIM A FEMALE GREAT DANE. ALL HE NEEDED NOW WAS SOME CLOTHESLINE.

BUT WHAT ABOUT THE GUARD DOGS?

THE DOGS FORGOT ALL ABOUT GUARD DUTY.

THE LIGHTS WERE OUT. NO ONE WAS HOME.

TEN MINUTES LATER, HE WALKED OUT WITH $30,000 WORTH OF JEWELRY.

THE FINAL SCORE
The end of an illustrious career

The burglary that ended Arthur Barry's career took place on May 29, 1927, in a part of Long Island known as King's Point. Barry had been tipped off that a large consignment of jewels had just been shipped to the palatial residence of one J. Lauriston Livermore. Livermore was a multimillionaire businessman who had recently divorced his first wife, and his new "trophy wife," half his age, was obsessed with diamonds. If she didn't get a fistful of new diamonds every few months, she became very cranky. So Livermore would order in trays of diamonds from jewelry stores "on approval"—whichever ones his wife liked, Livermore bought; the rest he sent back.

This latest consignment was easily worth over a million dollars, Barry's informant said. It was being kept in a vault in the furs closet of the Livermores' master bedroom. But they'd been there for several days already, so Barry would have to hurry.

During his decade-long career as a second-story man, Arthur Barry committed more than a thousand burglaries. His thefts were estimated by insurance company agents to exceed $10 million in total—averaging over a million dollars a year. And this was in the 1920s, when a dollar was enough to buy you an entire meal.

With his new assistant, Monahan, Barry arrived at the Livermore estate just after dark and found the Livermores having dinner—with guests.

"We'll just have to wait them out," he decided.

At about 9:00 p.m., the two couples (the guests were later identified as Mr. and Mrs. Henry Aronsohn) headed up to their bedrooms. But the lights didn't go out. Fifteen minutes later, everyone appeared at the front door dressed in elegant evening wear, the women sparkling with jewelry, and drove off in the Livermores' limousine.

"Damn," Barry swore softly.

He'd been studying the two couples with a small pair of binoculars. Livermore's wife had been wearing half a vaultful of jewelry, and Aronsohn's wife had been similarly decked out. This meant that much of what they had come to steal was now in a limousine headed for New York.

The robbers decided to wait for the partiers—and their jewels—to come home. But it was more than three hours before the limousine returned. And still the Livermores and their guests weren't ready for bed. For two more hours they sat up, drinking nightcaps and chatting.

Barry and Monahan hid outside in the shrubbery, shivering.

Barry was regretting he'd ever agreed to this job. Not so much because of the delays and the cold, but because he'd also agreed to do this one "live"—to make it a holdup rather than a simple burglary when no one was home. That part was Monahan's idea: if the diamonds were sitting in Livermore's safe, wouldn't they need Livermore's cooperation to open it up? After all, they weren't safecrackers.

When the last lights finally went out, it was three in the morning.

THE BURGLARS WENT BACK TO THEIR CAR FOR A LADDER.

THE ARONSOHNS DIDN'T WAKE UP UNTIL MONAHAN SWITCHED ON THE LIGHT.

DON'T BE ALARMED. WE WON'T HARM YOU. WE'RE JUST HERE FOR YOUR JEWELS.

On the dressing table Barry found earrings, pendants, and a diamond bracelet that Mrs. Aronsohn had worn that evening. He pocketed them all.

"I think I'm going to faint," Mrs. Aronsohn exclaimed.

"Oh, don't do that," Barry urged. "Would you like an aspirin?"

Barry helped her out of bed, took her to the bathroom, found her some aspirin, and poured her a glass of water. "Now just relax," he said. "All right?"

While Monahan kept an eye on the Aronsohns, Barry found a man's watch.

"Oh, please don't take that," Mr. Aronsohn said. "I got that from my mother. It's not worth much—it's just nickel-plated, not platinum."

"Keep your voice down," Barry said, dropping the watch into his bag. "We've got a couple of lookouts in the yard who'll start shooting if they think there's trouble."

After cutting the bedside telephone cord with a pair of clippers, he left the couple under Monahan's guard while he slipped down the hall to the Livermores' bedroom. Their door, however, was locked. Returning to the guest bedroom, he ushered the Aronsohns back into bed and locked the bedroom door. "Now don't make any noise or our men will shoot," he reminded them. "We'll leave your door keys with the Livermores; they'll free you in the morning."

Then the two burglars climbed back down their ladder and moved it quietly over to the Livermores' bedroom window.

From shelves and drawers, Barry grabbed diamond rings, cufflinks, necklaces, pendants, and bracelets—at least a hundred thousand dollars' worth.

He turned to Livermore. "Now the vault," he said.

"But there's nothing in it," Livermore said. "And anyway, it's jammed."

"I'm inclined to believe you, but I'd like to have a look inside anyway," Barry said, and pulled out his pistol again. "And I really must insist, Mr. Livermore."

Livermore very reluctantly handed over the combination. "Try it yourself," he muttered.

Barry clicked in the numbers, then pulled at the door. Nothing happened. He did it again. Still nothing. "We're going to need a hammer," he said to Monahan. Monahan disappeared down the ladder.

WHILE THEY WAITED FOR MONAHAN, THE BREEZE FROM THE OPEN WINDOW BEGAN TO GET CHILLY.

WOULD THIS HELP?

OH! HOW VERY KIND!

THIS MAY TAKE AWHILE. ANYONE FOR A DRINK?

YOU ARE A DEVIL, AREN'T YOU!

Monahan returned, hefting a small sledgehammer he'd found in the Livermore garage. After Barry finished his drink, he turned his attention to the safe.

"Please stand back a little," he cautioned Mrs. Livermore, who had moved closer to watch. "There might be flying chips."

He struck the spindle, hard. It flew off in a high arc, clattering to the floor. He got a firm grip on the door handle and pulled sharply. The door swung open.

Empty.

"What did I tell you?" Livermore sneered. "There *were* jewels in there last week—a big consignment from New York. But I sent them back a few days ago." He seemed hugely pleased.

Barry went back to searching the room.

"Now what are you looking for?" Mrs. Livermore asked.

"Cash," Barry said.

"Why don't I just show you where it is?" she said.

Jesse Lauriston Livermore—known as the "the Boy Plunger" for his daring stock market gambles—made and lost several fortunes over the course of his investment career. His second wife, Dorothy, was a former Ziegfeld Follies showgirl with a taste for Livermore's deluxe lifestyle: fully staffed mansions around the world, chauffeured limousines, and yachts—nothing but the best for the Livermores.

She went to a closet and opened a small drawer under a shelf of women's hats. She pulled out the cash—several hundred dollars' worth—and presented it to Barry.

"You're not really going to take this, are you?" she said. "It's my spending money."

Barry was looking at her collection of hats. "No, you keep it," he said finally. "I like your taste in hats. Buy yourself some new veils to go with them."

Monahan was standing there shaking his head. "Let's go," was all he said.

Mrs. Livermore touched Barry's arm. "You know that diamond and sapphire ring you took?" she said. "It was a present from my husband. Could I possibly have that back?"

Barry looked at her for a long moment, then pulled a handful of jewels out of his pocket and gave her back the ring.

"And also my husband's?" she said. Her look was apologetic. "They were a matched set, you see."

Barry grimaced and gave her that ring, too. Then he dug into his other pocket and pulled out Aronsohn's watch.

"You might as well give this watch back to your house guest," he said, handing it to Livermore. "It *is* platinum, not nickel-plate. Tell him he should learn the difference."

He waved and then disappeared down the ladder.

THE TAKEDOWN
The revenge of a woman scorned

A week later, with the newspapers still full of reports about the Livermore robbery, Barry decided it might be safer to get out of town for a while. On their way to the train station, he and his girlfriend Anna met Monahan at a drugstore, where Monahan passed Barry a small leather pouch containing the last few Livermore jewels he hadn't yet been able to sell. They agreed that Barry would hold on to them until he got back.

For some reason, their train kept encountering delays, and the short trip up to Lake Ronkonkoma ended up taking almost four hours. At one point, when the train once again stopped for no obvious reason, Barry suggested they get off and take a cab to the lake—they were only a few miles away. But Anna took too long to decide, and the train began moving again.

IT WAS A FATEFUL ERROR.

It turned out that Monahan and his wife had been having marital problems, and his wife had betrayed her husband and his partner to the police. The train's delays had been orchestrated by the police so detectives could get to the Ronkonkoma Station to arrest Barry. They found the Livermore jewels in his pocket.

In the end, it was his agreement to rob the Livermores "live" that proved his undoing. Though Barry had always been careful and had no criminal record, the couple had no trouble identifying him as their thief in a police lineup.

Barry was sentenced to twenty-five years in prison. He served nineteen years of his sentence, and was finally paroled in 1949 at the age of fifty-three.

Three years later, in 1952, Barry—by then the manager of a chain of dairy bars in Massachusetts—was asked by a parent-teacher association on Long Island to give an inspirational talk on "juvenile delinquency." In an effort to go straight, earn the trust of the community, and gain a reputation as an honest man, Barry had taken to accepting such invitations.

That evening, after his talk, a well-dressed, middle-aged woman came up to him. "Do you remember me?" she asked.

Barry looked at her carefully. "No," he finally admitted. "Should I?"

She smiled. "Let me help you remember," she said. "Do you recall an evening when you returned my spending money and complimented me on my taste in hats?"

Barry felt suddenly very moved. Dorothy Livermore had been his final victim—the last "client" of Arthur Barry, Master Jewel Thief. He supposed he should be angry with her; her identification of him in a

police lineup had cost him nineteen long years in prison. But he had always made his own choices, and borne the consequences. It was over now. He knew, suddenly, with a new certainty, that he would never be a jewel thief again.

Dorothy Livermore unclasped her hands. "I'm glad you're doing well, Mr. Barry," she said simply. "I'm *relieved* you're doing well."

He didn't move until she had disappeared through the door and out into the night.

THE GREAT TRAIN ROBBERY

No one believed it could be done ... until two rival London gangs joined forces and did it!

THE SCENE OF THE CRIME

A quiet night in Buckinghamshire

Just after midnight on August 8, 1963, a convoy of fifteen men in two Land Rovers and an army truck drove stealthily along the back roads of rural Buckinghamshire in southern England. A low-lying mist swirled around the vehicles, but the sky above them was clear and studded with stars. They were headed for the Bridego Bridge, a small railway overpass located about sixty-five kilometers (forty miles) northwest of London on British Rail's Glasgow-to-London line.

There was a military base nearby, and local residents were accustomed to seeing military vehicles patrolling the roads. The men in the trucks all wore army uniforms. No one would look twice.

THE ROBBERS

Two criminal masterminds are better than one

In the lead Land Rover, dressed in a major's uniform, was Bruce Reynolds, a tall, bespectacled man with a military mustache and the swashbuckling air of a paratroop commander. He was the leader of a gang of thieves known around London as the Southwest Gang (a.k.a. The Brighton Boys). Four of them sat squeezed onto the bench seat behind him. Four others followed in an army truck that was staying right on the Land Rover's tail.

The gang in the second Land Rover—known around London as the Southeast Gang (a.k.a. The Heavies)—was led by a short, fat man named Buster Edwards. Unlike the more sophisticated Reynolds, Edwards was a cheerful, hard-drinking, meat-and-potatoes man who spent his nights carousing and fighting in rowdy bars and nightclubs. He was warm-hearted, but he could be ruthless if necessary. His five men were all squashed into the Rover's rear seat and luggage compartment behind him.

THE HEIST

Bigger is better ... but the biggest is best

Teaming up was unusual for London's criminal gangs. Each gang controlled its own part of London, and kept a sharp lookout for rival gangs poaching on its territory. But this was a special job requiring a lot of smarts, technical expertise, inside information, and muscle—far too much for one gang alone. And Reynolds and Edwards had worked together before—they trusted each other.

When the vehicles arrived at the bridge, at around 2:00 a.m., they were quickly hidden in the nearby bush. Then the men pulled railway coveralls over their army uniforms. Now they looked like a team of railway workers on night shift.

Up on the rail bed, four sets of railway tracks glistened eerily in the moonlight. The only sound was the occasional bark of a dog from one of the farms nearby. In the distance, about a kilometer (half a

THERE WAS A SMALL UTILITY SHACK NEAR THE BRIDGE, WHICH EDWARD'S MEN BROKE INTO.

mile) up the tracks, four green lights glowed dimly, indicating that the lines were clear for all London-bound traffic.

Reynolds distributed two-way radios to a number of men from both gangs, and then he took two men with him up the track to the gantry. This was a narrow metal gangway built across the width of the rail bed at a height of about eight meters (twenty-five feet). It had a traffic signal (red, amber, green) hanging over each set of rails. Metal foot pegs enabled a maintenance man to climb up and walk across above the tracks, to service the four signals.

One of the men stayed at the gantry while Reynolds and the other man headed for a "dwarf signal" another kilometer (half a mile) farther along. This was a warning signal, intended to alert the engineer of a fast-moving train that a signal change was coming up at the next gantry. A lit-up amber light in a dwarf signal told engineers to slow their trains to a crawl.

Reynolds turned on his radio. "Can you hear me?" he asked in a low voice.

There was a small burst of static and then Edwards's faint response: "I hear you."

"We're at the dwarf, and I'm heading up to the next bend."

"Roger," came the brief reply.

Reynolds left his last man at the dwarf signal and continued up the track. Beyond the next bend, he'd be able to see any approaching London-bound train from several kilometers away.

Not long after he'd rounded the bend, he radioed a warning. "It's now 2:53, chaps. Only ten more minutes. She'll be coming through on Track Two."

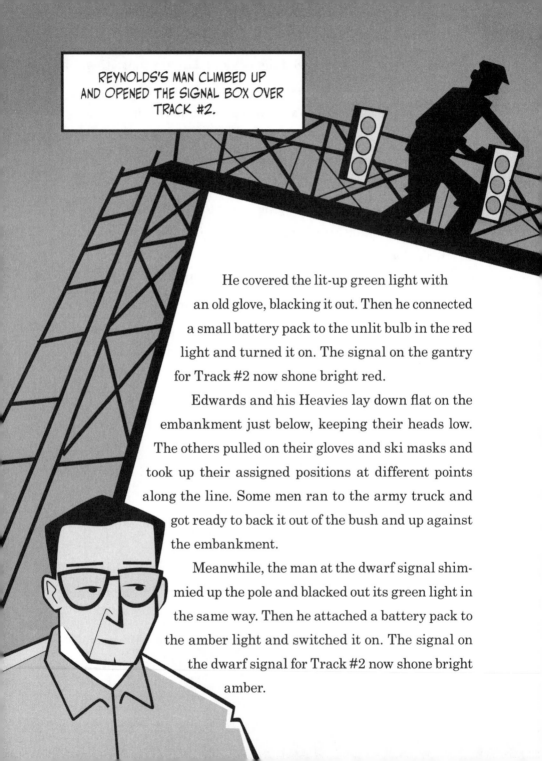

REYNOLDS'S MAN CLIMBED UP AND OPENED THE SIGNAL BOX OVER TRACK #2.

He covered the lit-up green light with an old glove, blacking it out. Then he connected a small battery pack to the unlit bulb in the red light and turned it on. The signal on the gantry for Track #2 now shone bright red.

Edwards and his Heavies lay down flat on the embankment just below, keeping their heads low. The others pulled on their gloves and ski masks and took up their assigned positions at different points along the line. Some men ran to the army truck and got ready to back it out of the bush and up against the embankment.

Meanwhile, the man at the dwarf signal shimmied up the pole and blacked out its green light in the same way. Then he attached a battery pack to the amber light and switched it on. The signal on the dwarf signal for Track #2 now shone bright amber.

At 3:02 a.m. everyone's radio crackled. "Here she comes, chaps," Reynolds's voice announced. "Get ready. This is it."

Soon the thrum of an approaching train began to vibrate through the tracks. Then they could hear it—a faint rumble approaching rapidly through the night, growing louder by the second. The ground began to tremble. A minute later the Glasgow-to-London Royal Mail train came thundering around the bend, its powerful headlight flooding the nearby forest with a brilliant intensity. A squeal of brakes indicated that the engineer had seen the amber dwarf signal ahead and had begun to slow down.

By the time the last railcar had passed the dwarf signal, the train was rolling along at little more than walking speed. At the gantry, the locomotive gave off an explosion of shrieks and hisses and came to a grinding stop.

The Royal Mail train now towered motionless above the gang, its engines throbbing. Trailing away into the dark was its long tail of cars, in which over seventy men and women in postal uniforms were busily sorting the mail, paying no attention to the train's stops and starts.

But the fireman in the locomotive wanted to know what the delay was about. He jumped down and headed toward a telephone box at the side of the tracks.

Back when trains had steam engines, the fireman's job was to stoke the fire that powered the engine. On a modern diesel locomotive, the fireman checks for dragging equipment or obstructions on the track, monitors the oil, temperature, and pressure gauges, and watches for the track signals that guide the engineer.

Edwards stood up and the fireman caught sight of him. "What's up, mate?" he asked.

"Problem up ahead," Edwards said, waving a piece of paper.

The fireman crossed the tracks to look—at which point the rest of the Heavies appeared and overwhelmed him. "Any noise and you're dead," Edwards warned the fireman, while two others quickly tied him up and dragged him down the embankment. The fireman made no effort to resist.

BACK AT THE LOCOMOTIVE, EDWARDS WAS STRUGGLING WITH THE ENGINEER.

ONE OF EDWARDS'S MEN RAN AROUND AND CLIMBED IN FROM THE OTHER SIDE.

ONE BLOW FROM EDWARDS'S BLACKJACK WAS ENOUGH TO SPLIT HIS SCALP.

Meanwhile, underneath the train, two Brighton Boys were disconnecting the couplings and vacuum hoses at the end of the second car. Their "inside man"—a postal employee known to them only as "the Ulsterman"—had explained that on Royal Mail trains the first car would contain regular mail, and no postal workers. Only the second car carried what they wanted: mail sacks full of money being shipped back to London from banks all along the line. There would also be half a dozen sorters working in it.

Edwards stuck his head out of the cab doorway. "You boys ready down there?"

"All clear!" came the reply.

Edwards turned to the engineer, who was sitting on the floor, wiping the blood off his face with his handkerchief. "You're going to move this train forward now to the bridge up ahead, and you're going to stop it exactly when I tell you to. You got that?"

The engineer nodded and stumbled over to the driver's seat. He turned several handles to release the brakes and pulled on the throttle. The engines burst into a roar.

But nothing moved.

Then suddenly there was a loud screech of metal as the accordion connection between the second and third cars ripped apart. Disconnected from the twelve other cars, the locomotive and its first two cars began to speed ahead.

"Now slow down, and stop right when we get to that shed at the end of the bridge. Right … now!"

The engineer reversed throttle and cranked on the brakes, and the train ground to a halt. Edwards climbed off.

AT REYNOLDS'S SIGNAL, THEY SMASHED THEIR WAY INTO THE CAR.

HVP STOOD FOR HIGH VALUE PACKAGE—MEANING MONEY.

THIS WAS THE HAUL OF CASH THEY'D COME FOR. REYNOLDS COULDN'T HAVE BEEN HAPPIER.

"All right." Reynolds grinned. "Let's get on with it. We're running low on time here, chaps."

Everyone quickly formed a human chain from the railcar to the army truck that had been backed against the embankment below.

The sacks were a lot heavier than they looked. Soon everyone was dripping with sweat, and some of the men were stumbling and falling. Someone got the bright idea of simply rolling the sacks down the embankment, but by the time Reynolds called a halt, several of the men looked ready for a heart attack. A few of the sacks had rolled off into the bush, but nobody had the energy to chase after them. Why bother when there were millions of pounds more in the truck? They had already loaded up 120 sacks full of banknotes. It had to be the haul of the century.

By the time they were ready to leave, the sun was almost up and the roosters on nearby farms were crowing. The men hastily pulled off their railway coveralls and became military personnel again. Someone hauled out a police radio and tuned it to the frequency of the Buckinghamshire police, but no word of the robbery yet.

Now the convoy was heading back the way they'd come, to Leatherslade Farm. This hideout, about fifty kilometers (thirty miles) away, had been bought for them by a crooked lawyer several months earlier.

The gang was obviously planning to be at the farm for quite a while: the police later found two hundred eggs, lots of canned food, and thirty-four rolls of toilet paper there.

THE VEHICLES WERE HIDDEN AT THE FARM.

EVERYONE KEPT THEIR GLOVES ON, TO AVOID LEAVING FINGERPRINTS.

REYNOLDS AND EDWARDS SAT DOWN TO TALLY THE TAKE. THE FINAL COUNT? £2.5 MILLION—£150,000 FOR EACH GANG MEMBER!

BREAKING NEWS

The police have their own theories

By the following morning, everyone had heard about the daring, precisely planned robbery. Radio announcers expressed amazement at the gang's sophistication and military precision. Crime historians couldn't remember a robbery in Britain that had ever involved so many criminals and so much money. The British Broadcasting Corporation was calling it "the crime of the century."

> People called in to their radio stations to express their outrage. The robbers had, after all, attacked one of the country's most sacred public trusts: "I mean, I can understand banks, or businesses, or maybe even the odd lorry [truck]," one caller protested. "But robbing the Royal Mail! That's right over the top, mate!"

The men listened to a barrage of bulletins and messages coming over the police radio. So far, the authorities were completely baffled.

By lunchtime, everyone was in high spirits, and when a radio station played Tony Bennett singing "The Good Life," everyone chimed in, clinking their whiskey glasses. Someone had brought a Monopoly set, and soon they were playing—using real money.

Reynolds had predicted that the police would assume the thieves to be Londoners, who would flee to their home base immediately after the robbery. That's why he had arranged for the purchase of Leatherslade Farm. But as the day progressed, it became increasingly clear that the police had assumed the complete opposite.

A house-to-house search was now underway in an ever-widening circle around Bridego Bridge. Clearly, it was only a matter of time before police arrived at the farm. Some of the thieves became panicky, and the group's discipline began to fray. They were supposed to be spending the next three or four days getting rid of the evidence—the mail sacks, the uniforms, the vehicles. The farmhouse had to be swept clean of fingerprints and other identifiers. But, by the end of the second day, most of the thieves had taken off.

The cleanup was now left to the lawyer who had purchased the farm for the gang, and he, for reasons that are hard to understand, decided to hire a man named Mark to do this very important job.

Either Mark didn't appreciate the urgency, or he wasn't told. But when Reynolds and Edwards met with the lawyer at his London office the next day to verify that the cleanup had been done, the lawyer admitted he had only just heard from Mark—and Mark *hadn't yet been out to the farm!*

DO YOU REALIZE WHAT YOU'VE DONE?

REYNOLDS AND EDWARDS RACED BACK TO THE FARM, HOPING TO AVERT DISASTER.

TRAPPED

Nothing left to do but run

It was too late.

As they were driving back, a news bulletin on the radio announced that police investigators had discovered the train robbers' hideout. At a place called Leatherslade Farm, they had found three military vehicles, a pile of partially burned and buried uniforms, and a large number of white canvas mail sacks filled with banknote wrappings.

Edwards turned to Reynolds. "I think we're bloody nicked," he said.

He was right. Although many of the gang members quickly fled England for places as far away as Australia, Mexico, Brazil, and Canada—and some even underwent plastic surgery to alter their appearance—they were picked up by Scotland Yard, one after another.

Fingerprint experts dusted the locomotive, the gantry, the vehicles, and the entire farm, and they found prints for almost everyone. Edwards was identified by a single print left on a banknote wrapper. Reynolds had left a fingerprint on the Monopoly board. Articles of clothing, keys—even a spot of paint on a shoe—brought down man after man.

By the middle of September—only five weeks later—five of the thieves had been arrested and warrants had been issued for five more. By year's end, nine were in custody, and by the following spring, when the first trials began, eleven men had been "nicked."

ON TRIAL
England's new media stars!

And now the robbers made their second big mistake—they became blinded by their skyrocketing fame. Media from all over the world had dubbed their heist "The Great Train Robbery."

Unfortunately for them, their trial was held not in London but in the town of Aylesbury, in Buckinghamshire, near where the robbery had been committed. And citizens there weren't as likely to be impressed by celebrities or their high-priced lawyers. The defendants ignored the judge, mocked the jury, and hammed it up for the press. They expected sentences of no more than five years, they said—ten at the most. Since little money had been recovered, the press drew the obvious conclusion: gang members expected to spend a few years in jail, then enjoy their ill-gotten gains in luxury for years to come.

It didn't turn out that way.

JOURNALISTS CAME FROM AROUND THE WORLD. IT WAS HARD TO GET A SEAT FOR THE SHOW.

ROGER JOHN CODREY WAS UP FIRST. THE ONLY GANG MEMBER TO HAVE PLEADED GUILTY, HE WAS EXPECTING THE MOST LENIENT SENTENCE. BUT THE JUDGE SAW THINGS DIFFERENTLY.

YOU HAVE BEEN CONVICTED OF A CRIME WHICH, IN ITS IMPUDENCE AND ENORMITY, IS THE FIRST OF ITS KIND IN THIS COUNTRY. I PROPOSE TO DO ALL WITHIN MY POWER TO MAKE SURE IT WILL ALSO BE THE LAST.

There were gasps throughout the courtroom. The lawyers were stunned, the press amazed. Even the gang members found it hard to look as if they didn't care.

And there was worse to follow. As gang member after gang member stood up to receive his sentence, the judgments came down like hammer blows: twenty-four years, twenty-five years, thirty years. In the end, eight of the accused gang members received sentences of thirty years. Most of the rest received twenty to twenty-five years.

THE JUDGE SENTENCED CODREY TO TWENTY YEARS.

THE TAKE

Easy come, easy go ...

By 1969, six years after the robbery, all but one of the robbers were firmly behind bars. The last holdout, Ronald Biggs, had been sentenced to thirty years as part of the first group of robbers to be tried. But he escaped from prison in 1965, and led Scotland Yard on a merry international chase that lasted an astonishing thirty-six years. Finally, in 2001, Biggs, too homesick to stay on the run forever, turned himself in and was sentenced to serve the rest of his original prison term—twenty-eight years.

Although Scotland Yard did finally catch all the robbers, it didn't do nearly so well with the money. In the end, only £200,000—a tiny fraction of the train robbers' haul—was ever recovered. For years, people wondered: what happened to all that money?

The answer is perhaps not too surprising: the gangs' lawyers got most of it. The trials lasted so long, and the appeals were so expensive, that much of the money was spent on legal defense.

And much of what remained—money the robbers had buried or entrusted to friends until their release—met with an even more ironic fate. It was stolen by other thieves while the train robbers were in jail!

So much for the old saying that there is "honor among thieves."

THE MANY FACES OF WILLIE SUTTON

When it came to bank robberies, Willie believed that charm, intelligence, and a lot of nerve were his best weapons.

THE METHOD

Fools rush in ...

Willie Sutton never took shortcuts. Most bank robbers in the 1920s barged in waving tommy guns and revolvers, but not Sutton. He was a professional and a perfectionist. For him, casing a bank was as important as actually robbing it. He never watched a bank from the same place twice—one day it would be his car, then a park bench, maybe a bus stop. And he changed his clothes and appearance every day. You never knew what might attract someone's attention.

It was this obsession with detail that made Sutton's robberies look effortless.

A TYPICAL HEIST
It's all in the details

For weeks during the fall of 1921, Sutton cased the Converse Bank in Long Island, New York. He approached all the banks he robbed—and there were many—in the same methodical way, carefully keeping a detailed record of when its employees arrived and what routines each person followed. He knew their names, as well as the names of their spouses and children.

The bank was opened each morning by a guard at 8:00 a.m. This guard then admitted the six clerks and tellers, who arrived around 8:15 a.m., identifying the employees through the windows in the upper part of the front doors. The manager arrived about fifteen minutes later.

On the day Sutton decided he was finally ready to rob the Converse Bank, he got up at 5:30 a.m.

FIRST, HE NEEDED HIS MAKEUP.

THE TRANSFORMATION

A whole new man

Sutton had always been fascinated by the theater, and after years of dating showgirls he had learned how to change his appearance—applying eyeliner, rouge, and charcoal—in a hundred different ways. Sometimes he added a mole or a scar. Sometimes he pushed small pieces of hollowed-out cork up his nostrils. He had boxes full of hairpieces, mustaches, eyebrows, and sideburns. He could make himself look years older or years younger, fat or thin, bald or hairy. The whole idea was to be unrecognizable if witnesses tried to identify him later in a police lineup.

Today he made himself look as young as possible because he was going in as a Western Union bank messenger.

Sutton's nickname in the bank robbing trade was "The Actor." He had become famous all over North America for his ingenious robberies using disguises. He had whole closets full of uniforms and costumes in his New York apartment that he used exclusively for bank robbing. His most common disguise was that of a policeman.

When his face was made up, Sutton selected a large briefcase and a neat-looking khaki outfit, inconspicuous and conservative, with a box cap—exactly what a bank messenger would wear. Then he steamed open a Western Union envelope containing a telegram he'd sent to himself the day before. He threw the telegram away, and substituted a similarly colored yellow sheet on which he'd typed the name of the Converse Bank's manager and the bank's address. He'd typed them so they appeared in exactly the right place in the envelope window.

Sometimes Sutton worked alone and sometimes he used helpers. For today's job, he had teamed up with Jack Bassett, a man who had joined him in a number of previous robberies. By 7:50 a.m., the two men were ready and waiting in a parking lot within sight of the bank.

Shortly after the guard entered the bank at 8:00 a.m., Sutton appeared at the front door in his disguise, briefcase in hand. He rang the bell.

The guard opened the door a tiny slit. "The bank's not open yet."

"Western Union," Sutton said. He spoke with a slight lisp, to confuse potential witnesses later. "Got a telegram for the boss."

Seeing the uniform and the envelope, the guard opened the door wider. Sutton handed him the telegram, a pen, and a small notebook. "Could you sign for it?"

The guard looked startled and took several bewildered steps back. Sutton quickly followed him in. At the same moment, Jack Bassett, who'd been waiting nearby, slipped through the door behind Sutton and closed it.

It was now 8:06 a.m.

Sutton took off his messenger's hat but kept the revolver cocked.

"I know you've got six employees who are going to show up any minute, Fred," he said to the guard. "Let everyone in exactly as usual. No funny business, or believe me, I'll use this." The guard looked at the gun and shrugged hopelessly. How did this bank robber know his name?

Bassett carried in half a dozen chairs and lined them up against the wall.

At 8:13 a.m., the bell rang for the first time. The guard looked through the window, then opened the door. The first clerk walked in. "Lovely day, Fred," he said cheerfully.

"That's what you think," the guard mumbled.

The clerk looked surprised—and then he saw the bank robbers. Before he could manage to react, Bassett took him by the arm, led him to a chair, and sat him down.

"Just sit tight and don't try anything," he warned.

The next arrival was a young teller in a summer dress.

"'Lo, Fred," she said happily, swinging her purse in circles around her arm. She stopped swinging abruptly.

Ten minutes later, the chairs were full.

AT 8:30 A.M., HARRY, THE MANAGER, ARRIVED.

RELAX, HARRY. I JUST NEED YOU TO OPEN THE VAULT.

THE BANK WAS DUE TO OPEN IN ANOTHER TWELVE MINUTES.

DON'T SUPPOSE I HAVE MUCH CHOICE ...

YOU'RE DEAD RIGHT ABOUT THAT.

BE A GOOD FELLOW, HARRY, AND OPEN THAT SAFE FOR ME?

THE TOTAL TAKE? ABOUT $250,000.

"Now here's the drill," Sutton explained when everyone was reunited in the lobby. "We've got a third member of our gang outside, with a rifle trained on the bank's front door. If anyone runs out that door during the next five minutes, he'll be shot. Everybody got that?"

Sutton knew perfectly well that the instant he and Bassett went out the door, the manager would be on the phone to the police. But it would take the police at least ten minutes to get there. That was all the time Sutton and Barrett needed to escape. He just didn't want anyone running after them, raising an instant alarm.

The bank employees obeyed his order. (They usually did.) At exactly 8:55 a.m., Bassett and Sutton slipped out the bank's front door and were quickly absorbed by the crowds on Jamaica Avenue.

Right on time. No violence. No hysteria. And a fat payoff.

It was a trademark Sutton robbery.

Sutton was known for his politeness during robberies. One witness said watching a Sutton robbery was like going to the movies—except the usher had a gun. Sutton did carry a gun, usually a tommy gun or a revolver, because, as he said, "You can't rob a bank on charm and personality." But, though his victims didn't know it, he never loaded his weapon—because somebody could get hurt. And—whether it's true or not—legend has it that he never robbed a bank if a woman screamed or a baby cried.

AN EARLY CAREER CHOICE
Lawyer or criminal?

Willie Sutton was raised in a rough part of Brooklyn. His father was a blacksmith and his mother was very religious. No one in the Sutton family had ever been in trouble with the police.

When Willie was a kid, his father was hit by a delivery truck that broke his collarbone. The driver was drunk, so his father hired an attorney and sued. The Sutton family expected to be well compensated for his pain, suffering, and medical bills. But before trial the attorney inexplicably settled with the insurance company for just a few hundred dollars. He convinced the family that they were lucky to get even that much. Later they discovered that the attorney had been on the insurance company's payroll—a common arrangement in those days. Willie wanted to become a criminal lawyer, to defend people like his father against insurance companies.

But a legal education was expensive, and Willie found himself working for pennies as a messenger boy in a bank. As he described it in his memoir, the poor customers would come in early in the morning to deposit their nickels and dimes.

THEN, ABOUT 11:00 A.M., THE BANK PRESIDENT WOULD DRIVE UP.

"NODDING AT EVERYBODY WITHOUT LOOKING AT ANYBODY—IT JUST INFURIATED ME," AS WILLIE LATER REMEMBERED IT.

WILLIE THE ACTOR
It's all about the costume

Willie began taking revenge by stealing rolls of postage stamps from his employer, but he soon progressed to much bigger thefts. One of his first teachers was a local safecracker and lock-pick. "Doc" Tate taught Sutton how to break into a safe by all the conventional methods of the day: picking a lock by feel, cracking it with a punch or jimmy, drilling it open—or, when all else failed, blowing it up with dynamite.

The problem was, the companies that manufactured safes kept improving their product. Their locks became increasingly more difficult to pick, cut, and drill.

One afternoon, as he was walking in New York City, Willie watched an armored truck stop in front of a bank. Two uniformed guards marched up to a secured entrance, rang the bell, and were promptly let in. A few minutes later, they emerged from the bank hauling heavy bags of cash.

After a dozen years of breaking, sawing, smashing, and blasting his way into banks, Sutton suddenly realized there was a far easier way to get the job done. *You just put on the right uniform!*

Bank employees were virtually programmed to view people in uniform as part of the team when they knocked on a bank door. A uniform announced the knocker's identity more loudly than any piece of paper or badge. In fact, Sutton suspected that the clerk who had let those uniformed guards into the bank hadn't even bothered to look at their faces. It was, Sutton discovered, one of the most basic tactics of the martial arts: using your opponent's unconscious reactions to defeat him.

Sutton discovered other advantages to this approach. Once you were inside the bank, a little psychology could take you a lot farther than a blowtorch or dynamite. There were at least three employees in every bank who knew the combination to the vault and could open it for you in just a few seconds. You simply had to come up with a convincing argument.

Ingenuity and psychology instead of brute force. Surprise and audacity instead of violence. These were the hallmarks of Sutton's style.

Next, Sutton rented a room in the theater district under the name of Waverly School of Drama. He sent out a request on letterhead to costume rental companies saying that the school was putting on a play and wanted to rent a policeman's uniform.

They all replied, eager to do business. All the Waverly School of Drama had to do was send their actors in for a fitting.

When he put on a policeman's uniform, he found himself checking the doors of the shops he was passing on his way to the bank, or waving to other officers on the street. When he put on the uniform of a mailman, neither snow nor rain nor heat nor hail nor gloom of night was going to keep him from delivering his special-delivery letter to that bank.

Once, when Sutton was disguised as a policeman and on his way to rob a bank in Philadelphia, a passing police captain stopped him and bawled him out for having a loose button on his collar. "The amazing thing was," Sutton recalled later, "I felt just awful about that button. 'Yes, sir, you're right, sir, it's an absolute disgrace, sir.' I found that the minute I put on that uniform, I was an utterly conscientious cop—right up until I got to the bank. Once I got to the bank, I stopped being a conscientious cop and became a conscientious thief!"

DRESSING FOR SUCCESS

It's all about the suit

Perhaps Sutton's most ingenious bank heist involving a disguise came in 1934, when he took aim at the Ozone Park Bank in Brooklyn. Casing the bank in his usual methodical way, he discovered two important facts. First, the manager looked surprisingly like Sutton himself. Second, the manager preferred double-breasted, gray pinstriped suits.

When Sutton finally decided how he would "take" this bank, he built his strategy around those two facts.

Instead of his normal method of hitting a bank *before* most of its staff had arrived, Sutton waited until the bank opened at 8:30 a.m., then walked in like an ordinary customer. He stayed just long enough to determine exactly what the manager was wearing, and how he was looking that day. Then he returned home.

As "The Actor," Sutton loved dressing up in uniforms and costumes—his repertoire included policeman, fireman, army officer, pilot, chauffeur, even window-washer. But his other nickname, "Slick Willie," came from his fondness for well-tailored suits and other elegant clothing. He was known as an immaculate dresser. In fact, when the FBI went looking for him, they distributed his "Wanted" poster to tailors as well as police departments.

THREE HOURS LATER, HE LOOKED JUST LIKE THE MANAGER.

AS SOON AS THE MANAGER LEFT FOR LUNCH, HE WALTZED IN AND HEADED STRAIGHT FOR "HIS" OFFICE.

FORGOT SOMETHING ...

WHEN HE LEFT, LESS THAN FIVE MINUTES LATER, HE WAS $100,000 RICHER. AND IT WAS ALMOST AN HOUR AFTER THE REAL MANAGER RETURNED BEFORE ANYONE REALIZED WHAT HAD HAPPENED.

ADDICTED TO ROBBERY
Willie strikes again ... and again!

By the time he was forty-five years old, Willie Sutton had been number one on the FBI's Most Wanted list for many years. He had been caught half a dozen times and sentenced to a total of almost one hundred years in prison. But he kept escaping and robbing more banks.

A psychologist at Sing Sing Prison had warned Sutton, "Banks will always present you with an irresistible challenge, Willie. You won't be able to walk past a bank without automatically starting to case it." And it was true.

"When all is said and done, I robbed banks because I really enjoyed it," he wrote in his memoir. "I was more alive when I was inside a bank, robbing it, than at any other time in my life. I enjoyed everything about it so much that no matter how much I scored, one or two weeks later I'd be out there looking for my next job. Even when it might cost me more than I could possibly hope to gain."

When it came to escaping prison, Willie Sutton applied the same principles of ingenuity, psychology, and audacity that he used in his robberies. Once, Sutton and two other prisoners, wearing stolen guard uniforms, took a pair of ladders and simply marched across the prison yard to the wall. When searchlights hit them, Sutton just hollered, "It's okay!" And no one bothered them after that!

In 1934, Sutton was caught, and he was sent to Eastern State Penitentiary to serve a fifty-year sentence.

For eleven years he tried desperately to break out—everything from swimming through the sewers to crawling through the heating ducts. Once, he and a dozen other inmates actually dug a long tunnel under the prison walls. However, when they finally surfaced, they found themselves crawling out *right beside a police car, with two officers in it!* Everyone was immediately recaptured, and Sutton was transferred to a higher security prison—from which he escaped in less than a month.

This time, Sutton was determined to stay out of trouble, and he soon got a job as a janitor at an old folks' home. During the seven years he managed to hide out there, Sutton really did make a serious effort to overcome his addiction to robbing banks. But so many thieves were now copying his famous bank robbing method that he was being blamed for all kinds of robberies he hadn't committed. He was sometimes even blamed for robbing different banks in different parts of the city at the very same time!

Finally he gave up. Why bother trying to resist? Sutton moved back into the city and began to case another bank—the Manufacturer's Trust on 14th Street and 10th Avenue.

It was the last bank he would ever case.

ON MONDAY, FEBRUARY 18, 1952, SUTTON WAS RIDING THE SUBWAY, PLOTTING HIS HEIST. BUT TO SOMEONE ELSE THAT DAY, HIS FACE LOOKED FAMILIAR.

HE WAS OUT OF THE SUBWAY AND ON THE STREET BEFORE HE REALIZED ANYTHING WAS WRONG.

HE HAD NO IDEA HE'D BEEN SPOTTED.

WILLIE ESCAPES AGAIN

A law student, at last

Sutton—arrested as an escaped fugitive—was brought to trial. The jury took one look at his astonishing criminal record and sentenced him to life in jail. This time he was sent to New York State's awful, riot-prone Attica Prison.

Given his sentence, Sutton might well have died in prison. But he didn't. He escaped once more—this time by applying his own bank robbing technique. He avoided digging, smashing, shooting, or brute force. He used ingenuity instead—and his opponent's unintended cooperation. He did it by studying the law.

Sutton pored over legal texts for seventeen years before he finally found the technicality that allowed him to appeal his life sentence and have it reduced to time already served. Nobody believed he'd be able to win, but with the help of several dedicated lawyers he was released in 1969, at the age of sixty-eight.

Sutton became famous for answering, when asked by a reporter why he robbed banks, "Because that's where the money is!" But Sutton claimed that he never said those words. What he did say was, "Go where the money is ... and go there often!" Perhaps his best piece of advice, though, was this: "If I could somehow persuade just one kid that crime is for suckers, I would feel that my life hadn't been completely useless. You can't win at crime. As you can see, I know."

Sutton never returned to bank robbing—he was too sick, weak, and tired. He was also broke. (He never revealed what happened to all that hidden loot.)

During the final eleven years of his life, before he died in 1980 at the age of seventy-nine, he was a poor but free man.

Sutton earned a modest living as a bank's security consultant, advising his former victims on how to avoid being robbed. He even made a series of television commercials, promoting the credit cards of the New Britain Bank & Trust Company in Connecticut. Called "the Face Card," it was among the first to carry the holder's photograph.

BIBLIOGRAPHY

Introduction

Cassie Chadwick: *Scoundrels & Scalawags*. New York: The Reader's
     Digest Assoc., 1968.

Jimenez Moreno: McCormick, Donald. *Taken for a Ride*. Blandford,
     UK: Harwood-Smart Books, 1976.

Soapy Smith: Collier, W.R. *The Reign of Soapy Smith*. New York:
     Doubleday, Doran & Co., 1935.

Joe Weil: Brannon, T. *"Yellow Kid" Weil: Con Man*. New York:
     Pyramid Books, 1957.

Billy Miner: MacPherson, M.A. *Outlaws of the Canadian West*.
     Edmonton: Lone Pine Publishing, 1999.

Ned Kelly: Brown, Max. *Australian Son: The Story of Ned Kelly*.
     Melbourne: Georgian House, 1956.

Charles-Hippolyte Delperch de la Bussière: Llewellyn, Sam. *Small
     Parts in History*. New York: Barnes & Noble, 1992.

On the Run with Mona Lisa

Esterow, Milton. *The Art Stealers*. New York: Macmillan, 1973.

McMullen, Roy. *Mona Lisa: The Picture and the Myth*. Boston:
     Houghton Mifflin, 1975.

Reit, Seymour. *The Day They Stole the Mona Lisa*. New York:
     Summit Books, 1981.

Blowing the Vault at Laguna Niguel

Rosberg, Robert. *Game of Thieves*. New York: Arno Press, 1980.

Steele, Sean. Heists: *Swindles, Stickups, and Robberies That
     Shocked the World*. New York: MetroBooks, 1995.

Take the Money and Fly

Gunther, Max. *D.B. Cooper: What Really Happened*. Chicago:
     Contemporary Books, 1985.

Himmelsbach, Ralph. Norjak: *The Investigation of D.B. Cooper*. West Linn, OR: Norjak Project, 1986.

Rhodes, Bernie. *D.B. Cooper: The Real McCoy*. Salt Lake City: Univ. of Utah Press, 1991.

The Napoleon of Crime

Macintyre, Ben. *The Napoleon of Crime*. New York: Delta Books, 1998.

www.crimelibrary.com/gangsters_outlaws/cops_others/worth/1.html?sect=13

Banknotes from Heaven

McClement, Fred. *Heist*. Toronto: Paperjacks, 1980.

"Loot From Larder Lake Bank Robbery Recovered." *The Northern News*, Kirkland Lake. July 21, 1949.

"Robbers of the Larder Lake Bank Sentenced." *The Northern News*, Kirkland Lake. August 4, 1949.

The Classiest Thief in Manhattan

Hickey, Neil. *The Gentleman Was a Thief*. New York: Holt, Rinehart and Winston, 1961.

The Great Train Robbery

Read, Piers Paul. *The Train Robbers*. Philadelphia: J.B. Lippincott, 1978.

Delano, Anthony. *Slip-up—Fleet Street, Scotland Yard and the Great Train Robbery*. New York: Fitzhenry & Whiteside, 2004.

The Many Faces of Willie Sutton

Sutton, Willie. *Where the Money Was: The Memoirs of a Bank Robber*. New York: Viking, 1976.

Reynolds, Quentin, and Willie Sutton. *I, Willie Sutton*. (reprinted) New York: Da Capo Press, 1993.

INDEX

Apollinaire, Guillaume, 22
Ariel, Washington, 55
Aronsohn, Henry, 116–118, 122
Attica Prison, 160

Barry, Arthur, 112–115, 118,
    119, 121–125
Bassett, Jack, 147, 148, 150
Biggs, Ronald, 143
Bridego Bridge, 126, 138
Brighton Boys, The, 127, 134
Bullard, Charley, 80, 81, 84

Carnegie, Andrew, 2
Cartier of Paris, 105, 108, 111
Chadwick, Cassie, 2
Chaplin, Charlie, 104
Chaudron, Yves, 25–27
Clara, 59, 60, 62–66, 68, 69
Clark County, 60
Codrey, Roger John, 142
Converse Bank, 145, 146
Cooper, D.B., 54, 55, 57–62, 64,
    65, 67
Cooper, Dan, 50–54, 57, 59–62, 68
Cotton, Paul, 59, 63, 65, 66, 68
Curtin, Johnny, 81, 83–85

Da Vinci, Leonardo, 10, 11, 26
De Valfierno, Eduardo, 25–27
Desmarais, Victor, 91, 93, 95–101
Dinsio, Amil Alfred, 29–37,
    39–44, 46, 47
Donahue, James, 104, 105
Donahue, Mrs. Jessie, 104, 105,
    109, 111
Doyle, Arthur Conan, 89

Edward Grey, 84
Edwards, Buster, 127–130,
    132–134, 137, 139, 140
Elliott, Little Joe, 78, 84

FBI, 29, 44, 46, 47, 50–52, 54–57,
    64, 69
Fitzgerald, F. Scott, 104
Flynn, Kitty, 76, 86

Gainsborough, Thomas, 73, 74
Gary, Albert, 93
Georgiana, Duchess of Devonshire,
    71, 73, 75–79, 84–89
Geri, Alfredo, 20, 22
Gervanni, Toni, 94–96, 99
Great Train Robbery, The, 141
Gunther, Max, 59, 69

Heavies, The, 127, 130, 132
Henne, Dutch Alonzo, 81, 83, 84
Holmes, Sherlock, 89
Hood, Robin 4, 5

Imperial Bank of Canada, 90
Ingram, Brian, 58

Jonkin, Tom, 103

Kelly, Ned, 4
Kingston Penitentiary, 102

Laguna Niguel, 28, 32, 44, 46
Lake Ronkonkoma, 123
Lamont, Jack, 96, 97, 99
Lancelotti brothers, 6, 7, 11, 13,
    16, 18, 24

Larder Lake, 90–92, 99–103
Leatherslade Farm, 136, 138, 140
Lewis River, 60
Livermore, J. Lauriston, 115, 118, 119, 121–124
Livermore, Mrs. Dorothy, 121–125
Louvre, The, 6, 7, 12, 16, 17, 19, 24, 25, 27

Manufacturer's Trust, 158
Martial, Leo, 91, 93, 95, 97, 101
Mona Lisa, 6, 10, 11, 13, 14, 17–20, 22, 24–27
Monahan, 116–124
Moriarity, James, 89

"Napoleon of Crime," 70, 74, 86
New York Times, 111
Nixon, Richard, 44
Northwest Airlines, 48, 50
Nyrop, Donald, 50

Ozone Park Bank, 155

Paul, Ralph, 99, 101
Perugia, Vincenzo, 6, 7, 9, 11, 13, 16–20, 22–24, 27
Phillips, Jack "Junka", 84
Picasso, Pablo, 22
Pinkerton Agency, The, 73, 77, 78, 111
Pinkerton, William, 77–79, 87–89
Plaza, The, 104–106
Poggi, Giovanni, 20, 22
Prison de Louvain, 80, 84

Reynolds, Bruce, 127–131, 135–140
Rockefeller, Percy, 113
Royal Mail train, 131, 132, 134, 138

Schaffner, Florence, 48, 49
Scotland Yard, 73, 75, 78, 79, 143
Scott, William (Captain), 49, 52, 53, 55, 60
Signore, The, 18, 19, 25
Smith, "Soapy," 3
Southeast Gang, 127
Southwest Gang, 127
Sutton, Willie, 144–148, 150–161

Tate, "Doc," 152

Uffizi Gallery, 20

Waverly School of Drama, 153
Weil, Joe ("The Yellow Kid"), 5
Western Union, 146
Westlake, Lloyd (Constable), 99
Worth, Adam, 74–89

FURTHER READING

Blundell, Nigel. *The World's Greatest Crooks and Conmen*. London: Octopus, 1982.

McClintick David. *Stealing From the Rich*. New York: M. Evans & Company, 1977.

Marzano, Tony, and Painter Powell. *The Big Steal*. Boston: Houghton Mifflin, 1980.

Robertson, Heather. *Ken Leishman, Canada's Flying Bandit*. Halifax, NS: Lorimer, 1981.

Rose, Colin (ed.). *The World's Greatest Rip-Offs*. New York: Sterling Publishing, 1978.

Spaggiari, Albert. *Fric-Frac: The Great Riviera Bank Robbery*. Boston: Houghton Mifflin, 1979.

Weston, Greg. *The Stopwatch Gang*. Toronto: Macmillan, 1992.

ABOUT THE AUTHOR & ILLUSTRATOR

Photo by Laura Sawchuck

Andreas Schroeder is the author of more than two dozen books, and has earned award recognition for his fiction, nonfiction and investigative journalism. He has written several books for children and adults on the subject of hoaxes. For 12 years, he also reported on swindles and deceptions for a popular national radio program.

Rémy Simard is a cartoonist, commercial artist, and award-winning author and illustrator. His work has appeared in a wide variety of books, magazines, and newspapers. He lives in Montreal, Quebec.